THE ARAB OF THE FUTURE

A GRAPHIC MEMOIR

A Childhood in the Middle East (1978–1984)

RIAD SATTOUF

TRANSLATED BY SAM TAYLOR

METROPOLITAN BOOKS HENRY HOLT AND COMPANY NEW YORK

Metropolitan Books
Henry Holt and Company, LLC
Publishers since 1866
175 Fifth Avenue
New York, New York 10010
www.henryholt.com

Originally published in France in 2014 by Allary Éditions.

Library of Congress Cataloging-in-Publication Data

Sattouf, Riad, author.
[Arabe du futur. English]
The Arab of the future : growing up in the Middle East (1978–1984) : a graphic memoir / Riad Sattouf ; translated from the French by Sam Taylor.
pages cm
ISBN 978-1-62779-344-5 (hardback)—ISBN (invalid) 978-1-62779-345-2 (electronic book)
1. Sattouf, Riad—Childhood and youth—Comic books, strips, etc. 2. Cartoonists—France—Biography—Comic books, strips, etc. 3. Middle East—Biography—Comic books, strips, etc. 4. Graphic novels.
I. Taylor, Sam, 1970– translator. II. Title.
NC1499.S337A2 2015
741.5'69092–dc23
[B] 2014041152

Henry Holt books are available for special promotions and premiums.
For details contact: Director, Special Markets.

First U.S. Edition 2015

Designed by Kelly Too

Printed in China
10 9 8 7 6 5 4

CHAPTER 1

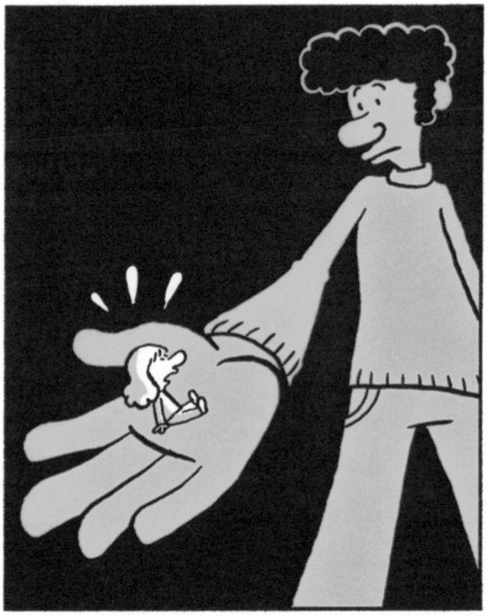

My name is Riad. In 1980, I was two years old and I was perfect.
Long, thick, silky, platinum-blonde hair
Golden highlights
Refined and delicate
Bright puppy-dog eyes
Lips made for suckling
Fresh off the tree
Back then, the world was one long procession of admiring giants.
What a cute kid!
Hey, gorgeous!
Everything that came out of my mouth was surprising and delightful.
GOOD-BYE.
So sweet!
Wow, he spoke to me!
He speaks so well!
All the women wanted to hold me in their arms.
How about I keep you for myself?
Me like you.
Total stranger
OH AREN'T YOU JUST DAAAAARLING!
I was awake for only a few hours a day, but it was enough: when it came to living, I was a natural.

I was my parents' only child and they worshipped me as well.
Clémentine, my mother
Abdul-Razak, my father
My mother came from Brittany and was a student in Paris. My father was Syrian. He came from a village near Homs.
Hi, how's it going? Can I sit with you?
UM, NOPE!
NO, THANKS.
My mother's friend
My mother
He was a brilliant student who'd won a scholarship to study at the Sorbonne. They met in the university cafeteria.
He's still there...
Ugh, what a bore...
This was the beginning of the '70s.
'Allo, I'm Abdel-Razak. And you?
Me? I'm nameless.
Yeah? I like that, is pretty. Is African?
And you? What's your name?
Like her. It's the same as hers.
Really?
"SAYMAZERZ!" That's really pretty! Is verry French? I'm...
Let's get out of here
Yeah.
Oh, OK. Coming.
No, you stay here. We just want to eat our lunch in peace.
Shall we mit up tomorrow?
Oh, sure, 7 p.m. at the Place de l'Opéra!
Yeah you will!
Great! See you tomorrow!
My mother took pity on him. She went to meet him in her friend's place.
Just coffee, that's it!
?!?

My father was writing his thesis on modern history. He came from a very poor Sunni family and he loved France.
France is wonderful! People can do whatever they want here!
They even pay you to be a student!
And they have Radio Monte Carlo...
It was 1971. Georges Pompidou was president.
The title of my father's thesis was "French Public Opinion toward England, 1912–1914."
With the French, they wanted not to have good terms with...
SHUSH! Hold on.
My mother was the one who typed it up, and she also made it intelligible.
"They broke off relations."
TAPTAP TAP TAP TATAP
Exactly!
TATAP TAP TAP
All his life, my father had been obsessed by the idea of being a "Doctor."
The best way to be a doctor is medicine... But I hate the sight of blood... It makes me sick!
So, because he was fascinated by politics, he chose to major in history.
History is best if you want to go into politics. This way, I might be president, ha ha!
I mean, who knows?
Hee hee!
In 1967, he had been devastated by the Six-Day War, when Egypt, Jordan, and Syria were crushed by the Israelis.
I would change everything in the Arab world. I'd make them stop being such bigots, get educated and join the modern world... I'd be a good president.
Then, in 1973, like all the Syrians of his generation, he managed to transform the Arab defeat in the Yom Kippur War into an "almost victory."
For two days, Egypt and Syria advanced into Sinai and Golan. The Israelis didn't know what hit them!
Then there was a cease-fire... And that's when the Israelis counterattacked, the cowards! We almost had them.
Next time, we'll finish them off!
Yet he had chosen to study abroad to avoid doing military service in Syria, which lasted several years.
Soldiers are morons!
I want to GIVE ORDERS, not take them!

1978 was the year I was born and my father defended his thesis. He finally became a doctor.
"Cum laude"? That's crap! No congratulations from the jury?
RACISTS!
THEY'RE RACISTS!
But it's good...
After eight years, "cum laude"! Racists!
After that he was a bit depressed for a while.
President Valéry Giscard d'Estaing and the First Lady visited a Renault factory in...
Pfft...
He listened to Radio Monte Carlo all day long, making comments as if he were part of the program.
Today Sadat, Carter, and Begin signed the peace agreement at Camp David . . .
Traitors
Egyptian scum.
Egypt has recognized Israel and . . .
In the end, to take revenge on France, he applied to several universities in other European countries.
Oxford has offered me a job as assistant professor.
Oxford!!! Wow, CLASSY!!!
This is Radio Monte Carlo. It's 4 p.m. . . .
They misspelled my name in the letter...
The PLO condemned the "Egyptian surrender" following the Camp David Accords . . .
...The Arab countries have unanimously rejected the Israeli Egyptian peace agreement The Arab League is weighing moving its HQ from Cairo to Tunis ...
YES! THAT'S MORE LIKE IT!
Then, one day . . .
I didn't tell you, but I applied for a job in Libya! And they want me! They're offering me a job as associate professor!
Look, they wrote "Doctor Abdel-Razak Sattouf" on the envelope!
?
The Ayatollah Khomeini has arrived in France, having been expelled from Iraq by Vice President Saddam Hussein ...
Ha ha! Khomeini in France! Serves the French right!
The Shiites, what a nightmare! But Saddam Hussein... I think he has a very big future! just like your daddy!
Goo!
WE'RE GOING TO LIBYA!

Paris
Odessa
Tirana
And so we left
Izmir
Ankara
Turkey
Malaga
Algiers
Tunis
Aleppo
Syria
Homs
Oran
Beirut
Damascus
Casablanca
Israel
Amman
Tunisia
Tripoli
Algeria
Benghazi
Jordan
Morocco
Libya
Egypt
Alexandria
My father believed in pan-Arabism. He was obsessed with education for the Arabs. He thought Arab men had to educate themselves to escape from religious dogma.
Look at this airport, built by Arabs!
Cigarette butts
I remember that when we arrived in Tripoli we were met by a bald man covered in warts. He was supposed to take us to our new house.
Welcome to our People's State, Doctor.
It was raining, and the entrance was chained shut.
Free of charge, of course! In our People's State, all housing is free.
Wet sand
Inside it was yellow, and water dripped from the ceiling.
Ah, it's nothing. It never rains. Anyway, it'll dry soon.
This is the "Little Green Book," where the Leader explains his vision of society and democracy.
You must read it.
It's truly a masterpiece.
Hang on, my brother, you forgot to give me the keys!
Keys? There are no keys. Look, there's no lock.
But there's a bolt you can close from the inside.

The Leader abolished private property, you see. In our People's State, houses are for everyone.
Your wife just has to bolt it shut during the day.
Everyone has a roof over his head here, Doctor. Nobody goes hungry, and everyone has a job...
Libya is the most advanced country in the world.
You'll figure it out soon.
Have a good day, Doctor.
As soon as the man had gone, my father put his fake leather briefcase on the table.
CLICK
He took out his lucky charm, a black plastic bull.
And placed it on top of the TV.
For my father, that always meant he was home.
A little later, the rain stopped and we went for a walk around our new neighborhood.
Look, Riad! That's Gaddafi. A great Arab president!
Abandoned building sites
Empty streets

My father took us to see the university, which was nearby. That, too, was yellow. It looked new, in spite of the cracks all over its façade.
?
No one around
Suddenly he noticed something. He started running toward a cluster of trees. He looked very happy.
?
CRACK
Lots of small, black, furry fruit fell from the tree. They were mulberries.
In my village in Syria, we called them "toutes."
My father crammed a dozen into his mouth. I could see the mashed-up fruit on his tongue because he never closed his mouth when he was chewing.
Afterward, he threw another stick at the tree...
...and let us taste them.
Hee hee
I've not had these in 15 years!

When we got back to the house, our bags were neatly arranged outside the door.
It's locked from the inside!
BANG BANG
Hello, brother. How can I help you?
Hello to you, brother. What are you doing in my house?
But, brother, this is my house. It was empty . . . The Leader gave all citizens the right to live in unoccupied houses, as you know.
What? Listen, I'm a professor at the university! I'm going to the police!
There's no point. I'm a policeman...
Just try a few doors, you'll find another house, my brother.
Good-bye, little girl!
When my father felt humiliated, he would stare into the distance with a little smile on his face and scratch his nose while he sniffed.
What are we going to do?
Sniff
Sniff
Sniff

At that age, I had great difficulty working out the difference between dream and reality, especially at night.
For instance, I'd be walking through candlelit hallways with no ceilings...
...when suddenly an incredible bull would appear.
Brrrgh!
I'd start to cry out, but no sound escaped my mouth. When I turned to flee, I found a second bull behind me, blocking my exit.
Brrrgh!
The two beasts were just about to skewer me on their horns...
...
...when a massive hand grabbed me at the very last second and pulled me up to safety.

It was my father's hand.
He put me back to bed...
...and carried on watching TV.
God is the greatest! God is the greatest! He is above the plots of the aggressors. And he is the best ally of the oppressed.
My father had found a tiny apartment in a ghetto for expatriates. It was practically deserted.
With faith and with weapons, I shall defend my country!
We all slept in the same room.
Sing with me! Sing with me! God is the greatest!
Gaddafi was on TV all the time.
Oh world, watch and listen! The enemy's army is seeking to destroy me!
He reminded me of me.
With truth and my pistol, I will repel them!
Like me, he had lots of people admiring him and smiling at him all the time.
Sing with me! Sing with me! God is the greatest!
I liked to watch him.
God is above any attacker! And if I die, I'll take the enemy with me!

My parents would fall asleep in front of the TV... Not me.
Hey!
Hey!
And then, like a robot, my father would start talking.
zzz... Once upon... a time... zzz.
Once upon a time, there was a little fox cub...
...who lived with his fox family. He had lots of brothers and sisters, and he was the youngest... zzz...
Yes? And?
. . . they lived in a hole without any light and they were all very hungry . . .
Grrr
Grr
Grrr
Grr
Zzzzzzzzz
And then what?
Then what?
...So they went out to hunt moorhens... But there weren't any... So they went further away... And they forgot about the little fox cub, who was left all alone...
Grr
. . . and he was so hungry . . . zzz . . . that he fell asleep . . . zzz
Then?
What?
What then?
And he would start over again at the beginning, repeating the story in a loop.

"The Green Book" by Muammar Gaddafi explained the Supreme Leader's opinions about everything.
"The house belongs to whoever lives in it," says Gaddafi.
Let's not ever leave this one, then.
In 1969, Gaddafi had overthrown King Idris I in a more or less bloodless coup d'état.
"Popular assemblies are false representations of the people. The very existence of a parliament presupposes the absence of the people . . ."
"So it is not reasonable that democracy should be merely the privilege of a small group of deputies who are supposed to act in the name of the masses. Power should belong entirely to the people . . ."
He's a cunning one!
Intelligent, you mean.
At first, Westerners liked him. He didn't interfere with their interests.
Ha . . . Listen to what he says about women . . .
Then he nationalized the oil companies, doubled salaries, turned palaces into schools, and made Arabic the language of the universities.
"Like a man, a woman is a human being. There can be no doubt on that score . . ."
Thanks a lot, Gaddafi!
He closed all the bars, night-clubs, cafés, and restaurants, which were now considered places of debauchery.
"According to gynecologists, women, unlike men, have a period every month."
Gaddafi claimed to be very devout. He supposedly lived in a tent and drank camel's milk every morning.
"Women are affectionate, beautiful... and fearful. In short, women are gentle and men are tough."
Does it really say that?

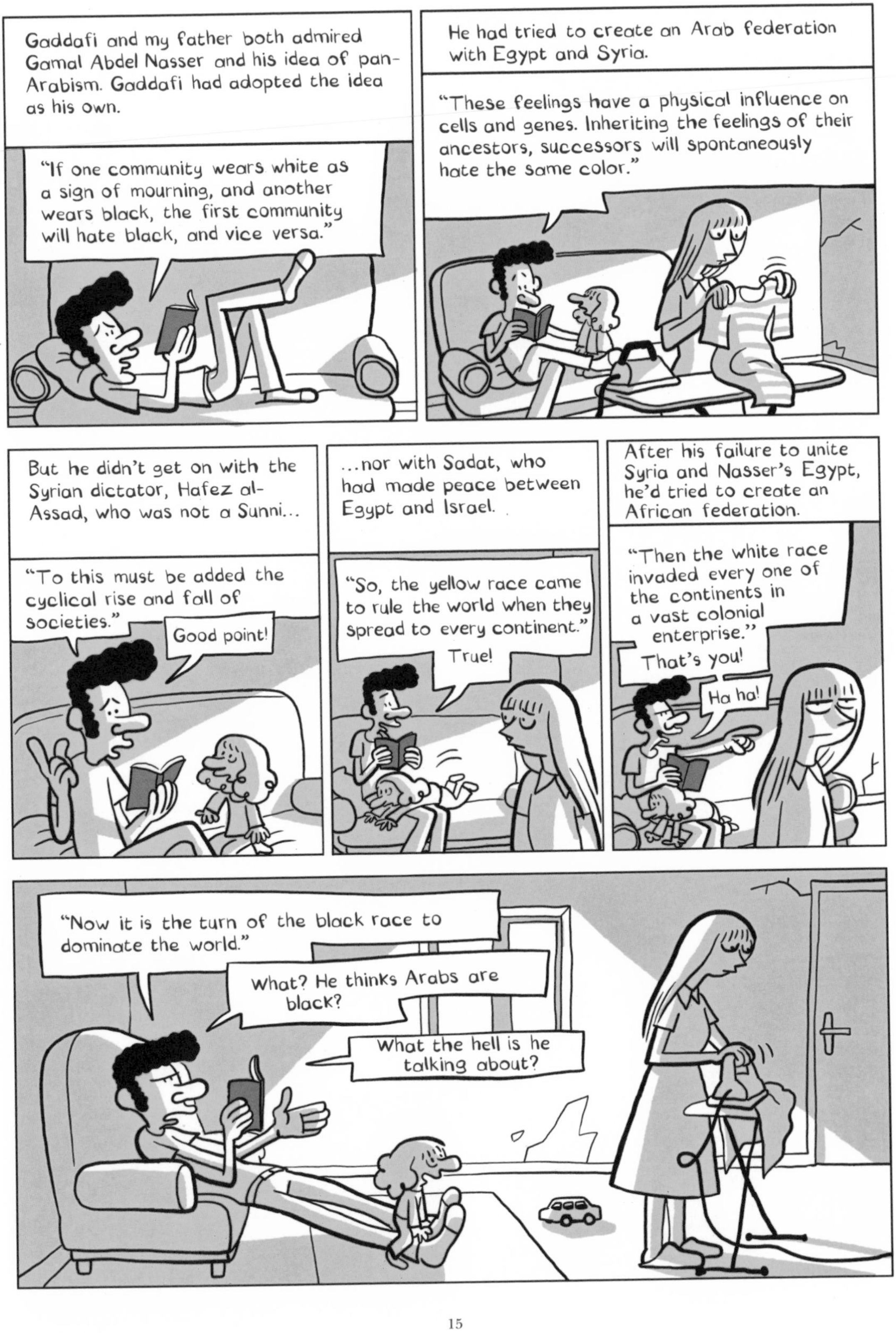
Gaddafi and my father both admired Gamal Abdel Nasser and his idea of pan-Arabism. Gaddafi had adopted the idea as his own.
"If one community wears white as a sign of mourning, and another wears black, the first community will hate black, and vice versa."
He had tried to create an Arab federation with Egypt and Syria.
"These feelings have a physical influence on cells and genes. Inheriting the feelings of their ancestors, successors will spontaneously hate the same color."
But he didn't get on with the Syrian dictator, Hafez al-Assad, who was not a Sunni...
"To this must be added the cyclical rise and fall of societies."
Good point!
...nor with Sadat, who had made peace between Egypt and Israel.
"So, the yellow race came to rule the world when they spread to every continent."
True!
After his failure to unite Syria and Nasser's Egypt, he'd tried to create an African federation.
"Then the white race invaded every one of the continents in a vast colonial enterprise."
That's you!
Ha ha!
"Now it is the turn of the black race to dominate the world."
What? He thinks Arabs are black?
What the hell is he talking about?

During the day, while my father was at the university, my mother and I guarded the apartment.
NO!
I just didn't bolt it!
Is this free?
?
I was allowed to play in the hallway.
I made two friends.
Adnan, from Yemen, who always looked sleepy
Abani, an Indian girl, who smelled funny
They had one thing in common— they were fascinated by me...
Vroom
Vroom
Vroom
Hey!
Hey!
...and especially by my blond hair. The Indian girl seemed mesmerized and spent all her time touching it.
You American? Americans have yellow hair. Yeah, I'm sure you're American!
Nanana
?
But whenever I spoke to Abani, she walked away from me...
You want to...
?
Nanana
...and started to giggle.
Hee
Hee
Hee
Hee

There always came a moment every day when Adnan would climb up on something dangerous.
He'd look at us casually...
Then he'd start up with the Libyan national anthem.
Oh world, watch and listen! The enemy's army is on its way, seeking to destroy me! With truth and my pistol, I will repel them!
We sang along at the tops of our voices.
Allah is above any attacker! And if I die, I'll take the enemy with me! Say with me, woe to the colonialist!
Eventually, his mother would come to fetch him.
Hnnn.
And soon after that, Abani's mother would come and get her daughter.
Pagana magané baligala!
Smells of incense and animal poop
Abani would start to cry. The two of them would leave without touching each other.
Tagabagani! Nagaloo nagani! Nagalani!
Waaaaaah
?
And sometime later, my father would come back from work.

We had to line up to get our food from a cooperative. Men went on one day and women on the next, to avoid "indecent" contact in the crowd.
Move, jerk-off!
Asshole!
Hurry up, dickhead!
Sucker!
Each group had its own special odor. The women smelled of dust and sweat.
Move forward, bitch!
Hurry up, you whore!
Back off!
The men smelled strongly of urine and sweat.
Jerk!
Asshole!
Big fat drops of sweat poured off of them.
GRTT GRTT
Hey, you, don't cut in line!
SHUT YOUR MOUTH, YOU SON OF A DOG!
YOU WANT SOME OF THIS?
SNIFF
SNIFF

Usually, we'd reach the counter after about an hour of this and hand over our coupons.
Here, your bread, 18 eggs, and three boxes of Tang.*
TANG
*Freeze-dried orange juice.
Haven't you got anything other than eggs? That's all we've had for two weeks... The kid can't eat just eggs all the time...
Give him some Tang, or tell your wife to give him her milk!
GET LOST!
But...
OUT OF THE WAY, YOU SON OF A DOG!
OW!
GET LOST, ASSHOLE!
On the way home, we stopped to see if there were any toutes.
My father hated wearing shoes.
When I was your age I used to go barefoot!
You want to try?
It's good for your feet.
We both had toes that were connected at the knuckle.
?

Here are some examples of offerings supplied by the Libyan People's State.
Six cans of corned beef
+
a very small bag of rice
Lots of grape juice
+
baked beans
BEANS
BEANS
Two pounds of sugar
+
another bit of rice
A bit of sugar
+
more corned beef
There was one time when we had bananas coming out of our ears.
My mother lost weight
More bananas.
YAAAAAY!
They were either green and hard...
At least he's eating...
Delicious
...or black and soft.
Mesmerized by the taste
C'MON!
HEY BITCH!
HURRY UP!
C'MON!
Oh no, not bananas again ...
Um... ONLY BANANAS?
Our Leader adores bananas, my sister! He says it's the fruit of the people.
YUM! YUM!

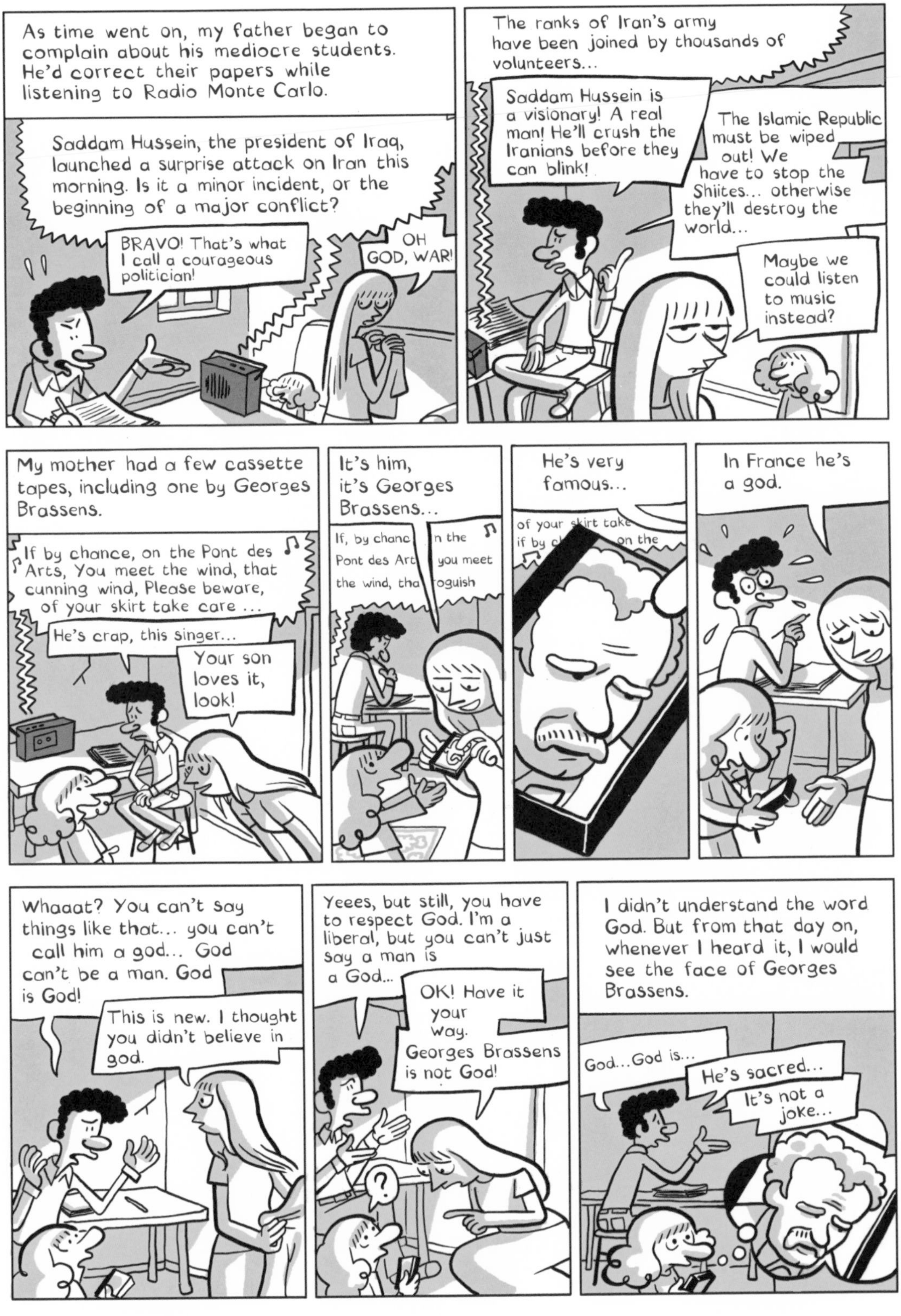

As time went on, my father began to complain about his mediocre students. He'd correct their papers while listening to Radio Monte Carlo.

The ranks of Iran's army have been joined by thousands of volunteers...

Saddam Hussein is a real man! He'll crush the Iranians before they can blink!

The Islamic Republic must be wiped out! We have to stop the Shiites... otherwise they'll destroy the world...

Maybe we could listen to music instead?

Saddam Hussein, the president of Iraq, launched a surprise attack on Iran this morning. Is it a minor incident, or the beginning of a major conflict?

BRAVO! That's what I call a courageous politician!

OH GOD, WAR!

My mother had a few cassette tapes, including one by Georges Brassens.

If by chance, on the Pont des Arts, You meet the wind, that cunning wind, Please beware, of your skirt take care ...

He's crap, this singer...

Your son loves it, look!

It's him, it's Georges Brassens...

If, by chance, on the Pont des Arts, you meet the wind, tha roguish

He's very famous...

of your skirt take if by ch on the

In France he's a god.

He's crap, this singer...

Whaaat? You can't say things like that... you can't call him a god... God can't be a man. God is God!

This is new. I thought you didn't believe in god.

Yeees, but still, you have to respect God. I'm a liberal, but you can't just say a man is a God...

OK! Have it your way. Georges Brassens is not God!

I didn't understand the word God. But from that day on, whenever I heard it, I would see the face of Georges Brassens.

God...God is...

He's sacred... It's not a joke...

Adnan, too, was enthralled by the abundance of bananas.
Bananas, they're the best thing in the world.
That's true!
LA LA LA LA
What about you, Abani? Do you like bananas, too?
LA LA LA LA LA
AGH
LA LA LA LA
HMPF
Abani never responded to Adnan. In fact, she never really looked at him, either.
Bananas are great!
Yes, they're the best thing in the world.
I think there's lots of bananas in heaven.
What's heaven?
It's a wonderful place where people go when they die. Life there is better than it is here.
It's the place where God lives. Bananas are so nice, I bet God eats them all the time.

Heaven is a garden where the sun always shines.
God sits in a big chair in the middle of the garden, and people must watch him while they eat bananas.
And us, too, we'll have to watch him when we go to heaven.
He'll smile at us and give us all the bananas we want. He'll never say to us, "No, that's enough, stop eating bananas."
And we won't even finish the one we've got before God gives us another one.
Come!!
Gaddafi wanted to educate the youth.
PAPA!
He had made an appeal to Arab-speaking university professors living abroad.
So, how's it going?
He'd offered to pay them in U.S. dollars if they came to teach in Libya.
Look, what a cute kid!
His hair is golden!
My father earned $3,000 per month, an excellent salary.
Come on, Adnan...

Back then, I didn't understand very much. But I was sure of one thing: my father was fantastic.
Watch! I'm just like McEnroe!
When he played tennis against the wall of our building, he sometimes managed to hit the ball right over the roof.
DAMN! Son of a dog!
WHACK
When I tried it, the ball didn't even reach the wall.
UNGH
He could get the ball up on the roof even without using a racket.
He was so strong, he could pick me up with one hand, as if I weighed nothing.
Come on, let's go look for the balls!
He could identify birds when they were flying.
Look, ducks! Ah, if only I had a rifle.
Look, storks! If only I had a rifle.
I bet they taste really good!
He was obsessed by the prospect of eating animals.
Have you ever seen a nest?
No. What's that?
It's a bird's house.
Smell of oranges!

He had fitted a lock to the apartment door. This was illegal, but he took the risk so we could all go out together for walks.
LOOK! THERE'S ONE UP HERE!
THERE'S A NEST! THERE'S A NEST!
There's no need to yell...
Come see! It's incredible.
It was very well hidden, but I found it.
Look, there's an egg!
Pick it up.
What is it?
An egg? Well, it's a bird's baby.
It's like you, you're our egg.
Where are the egg's mama and papa?
They're not here. They must be out shopping or something...
I'm going to leave the nest there, empty, like that.
We'll take the egg with us. We can eat it. Maybe it's a quail's egg.

When I asked my father to draw something for me, he always did the same thing.
Listen, I'm going to draw you the best car in the world: A MERCEDES.
Mgnmfssmgn...
He started to mumble
I'll have a Mercedes one day...
KRR
KRRR
He held his pencil incorrectly when he drew
KRRRRR
There you go: a beautiful Mercedes.

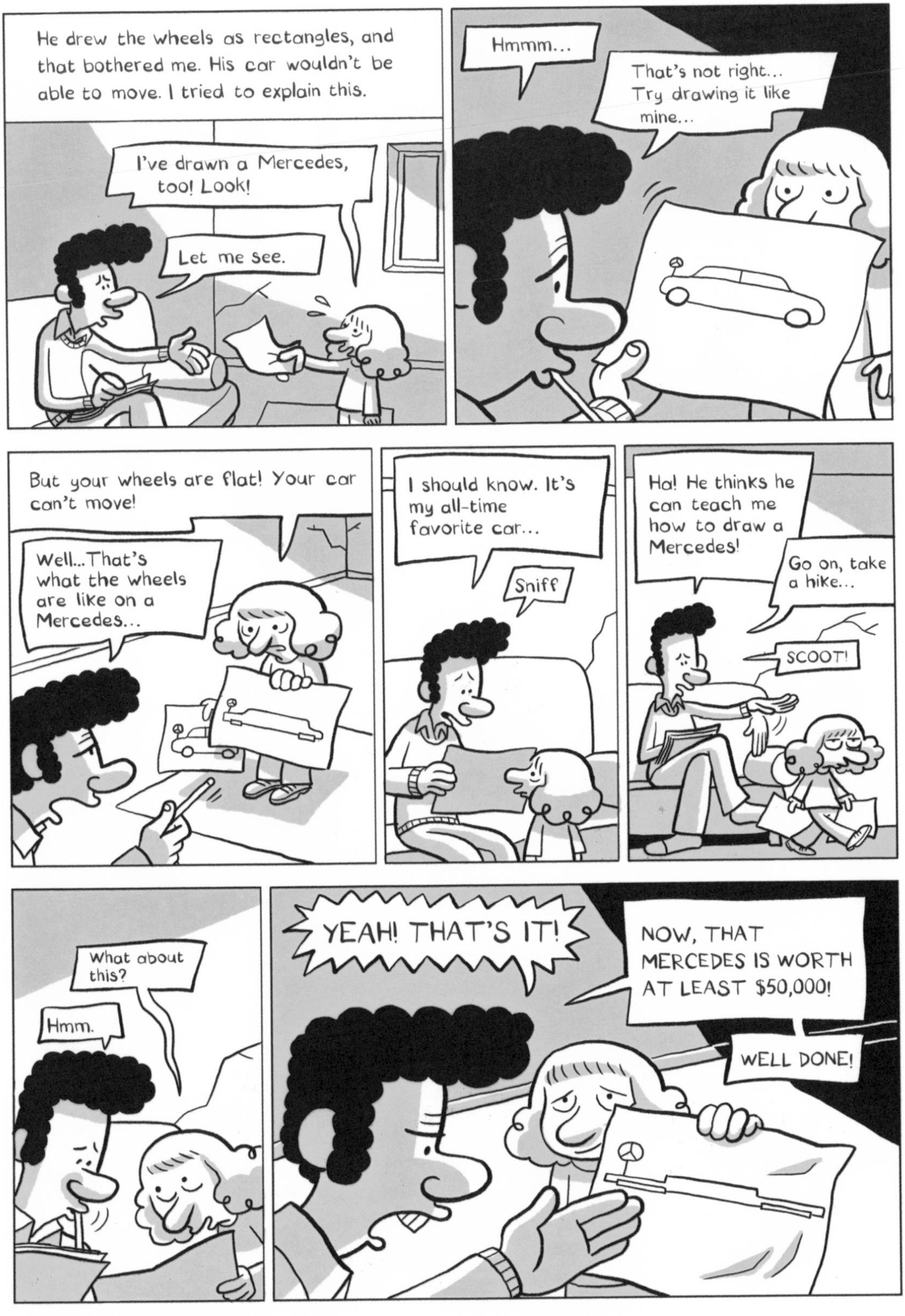
He drew the wheels as rectangles, and that bothered me. His car wouldn't be able to move. I tried to explain this.
I've drawn a Mercedes, too! Look!
Let me see.
Hmmm...
That's not right... Try drawing it like mine...
But your wheels are flat! Your car can't move!
Well...That's what the wheels are like on a Mercedes...
I should know. It's my all-time favorite car...
Sniff
Ha! He thinks he can teach me how to draw a Mercedes!
Go on, take a hike...
SCOOT!
What about this?
Hmm.
YEAH! THAT'S IT!
NOW, THAT MERCEDES IS WORTH AT LEAST $50,000!
WELL DONE!

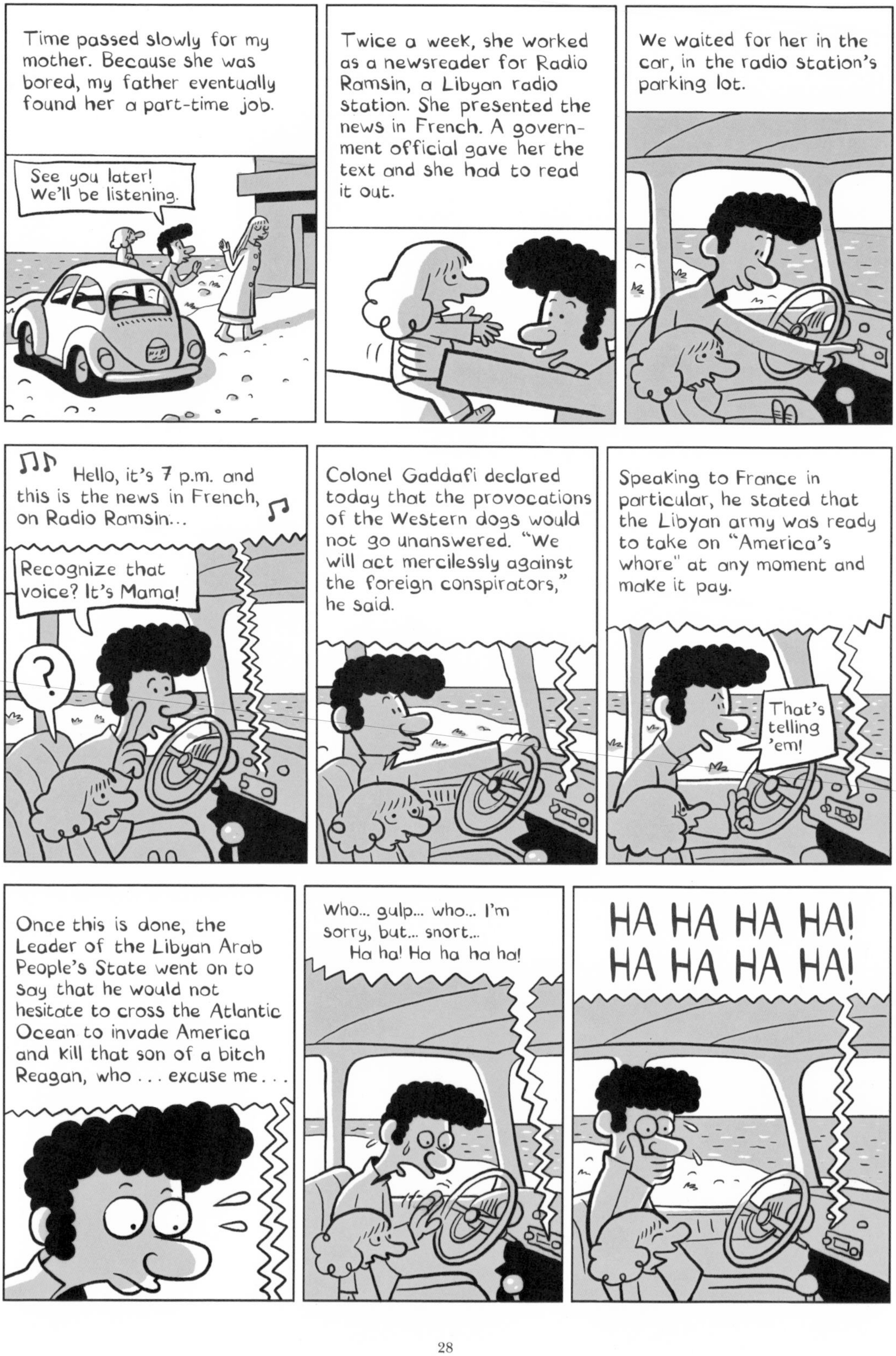

Time passed slowly for my mother. Because she was bored, my father eventually found her a part-time job.
See you later! We'll be listening.
Twice a week, she worked as a newsreader for Radio Ramsin, a Libyan radio station. She presented the news in French. A government official gave her the text and she had to read it out.
We waited for her in the car, in the radio station's parking lot.
Hello, it's 7 p.m. and this is the news in French, on Radio Ramsin...
Recognize that voice? It's Mama!
?
Colonel Gaddafi declared today that the provocations of the Western dogs would not go unanswered. "We will act mercilessly against the foreign conspirators," he said.
Speaking to France in particular, he stated that the Libyan army was ready to take on "America's whore" at any moment and make it pay.
That's telling 'em!
Once this is done, the Leader of the Libyan Arab People's State went on to say that he would not hesitate to cross the Atlantic Ocean to invade America and kill that son of a bitch Reagan, who . . . excuse me . . .
Who... gulp... who... I'm sorry, but... snort... Ha ha! Ha ha ha ha!
HA HA HA HA! HA HA HA HA!

After laughing hysterically on the air, my mother was summoned to a meeting with the head of the radio station.
He wanted to know if my mother had been laughing at the Leader's speech. That was very serious.
So, threats of war make you laugh, do they?
Sir, my wife doesn't speak Arabic, so I'm going to reply for her.
The reason she laughed is that the page she was reading from had been stapled the wrong way. She was surprised and had a fit of nervous laughter.
She's a woman... They're all a bit hysterical, aren't they? Ha ha...
AH! Let me see that...
It's her letter of resignation.
HMM.
HMM.
Would you agree to let your wife work on TV? She's a good presenter and she looks happy...
Um... No... No, definitely not. But thank you for asking!
What's he saying?
I just want my wife to stay at home... and look after my son...
I... I'm a professor at the university...
Hmm
Hm
That's a shame. The Leader likes to see Frenchwomen...
I... I work for the People's State...
I'm sorry. It was so stupid, what I had to say, that when I saw I couldn't read the page, I just lost it.
It doesn't matter. It's not like you were getting paid.

One day, we went to the airport. My father had put his suit on.
جمارك
HEY!
?
BANG!
OOOO-HHHH! OOOO-HHHH!
Look, this is MY mama!
And this man is my brother!
They smelled very strongly of sweat, but I liked it.
MWAH MWAH
I didn't understand anything they said.
What's she saying?
Bich be el bent!
Nothing. She says he's very beautiful, and that he looks like a girl with his long hair.
Li li li

My uncle's name was Mohamed, but we had to call him Haj Mohamed. That meant he had made a pilgrimage to Mecca.
My brother says he's the first Sattouf to have blond hair.
HMM
Shakaro asfar
He was very gentle and kind. He was older than my father and had lots of charisma.
WHOOO! WHOOO!
They hadn't seen each other for 15 years.
Hello!
HRRRK PTOO!
Back in our apartment, they moved into our bedroom.
I moved the bed out of the way. Your grandmother and your uncle are used to sleeping on the floor.
After that, they said their prayers. I didn't know what they were doing. My father started correcting his students' work.
My uncle mumbled things and stole sideways glances at me.
What he was doing seemed very important.
My father looked a bit embarrassed.

He was very happy to see his mother again. He turned back into a small child.
It's my mama!
This is my mamaaa!
Ahey! Ahey!
It's my very own mama! Ohh, ohh!
I kiss her feet!
Mwaah Mwaah! Ohh!
Oh! Oh! Oh! Oh!
Hada zghiri!!!
My uncle seemed shy around my mother.
Something to drink?
UH... AHEM...
What's up with him?
Ha ha... He thinks a man should not talk to any woman other than his wife. It makes him uncomforable...
Here, pass me the glass of water. I'll give it to him.
He's not used to seeing the long hair of a foreign woman...
My grandmother smiled all the time. Her eyes were small, piercing, and very clear.
She only liked sitting on the floor
She looked very carefully at everything.
But as soon as she felt anyone looking at her, she would stare into space.

They did nothing all day. They just waited around until my father came home.
Ohh ohh!
?
The building we lived in gradually filled up.
CLICK CLICK
It's taken!
We watched "Little House on the Prairie." I didn't understand a single word of it.
Neither did my uncle. His eyes would drift away from the screen...
...and he started to mumble. He looked preoccupied.
Mghmgn gnn...
In the evening, my father talked to them in Arabic. It was not the same Arabic as people spoke in Libya. I couldn't understand anything they said.
Shu? Howe Kaman maat?
Aiiie!
Heh
Heh
After dinner, he would put his mother to bed. He'd bought lots of blankets, which he piled up on top of her.
I think she'll be fine now!
I'm scared she'll freeze to death at night...
Her hair was jet-black

One afternoon, we went to visit Leptis Magna. The ruins of this Roman city are seventy-five miles from Tripoli.
The place was utterly abandoned.
A long time ago, lots of people lived here... They thought they were the most powerful people on earth!
And now look, it's just ruins!
Ha ha!
My uncle and my grandmother seemed ill at ease. They smiled far too much.
We won't stay here long. Haj Mohamed has never been this close to the sea. He doesn't really like it.
Don't look at them. Pretend I haven't mentioned it.
My uncle tried not to lose face.
He checked that no one was looking at him...
...and managed to keep his back to the sea.

Look at this pond! These are the glorious inhabitants of this city now: tadpoles!
What's that?
They're baby frogs. You can't eat them, urrghh!
Although... the French like eating frogs, actually! Ha ha...
Had sabei wala benet?!?
MWAH
We're going to have to cut your hair, I'm afraid.
You look like Brigitte Bardot!
Shufo hai haad haifi hala!
What's she saying?
My mother's saying she should shut her mouth, because she looks indecent like that.

A few weeks later... My uncle and my grandmother had gone back to Syria. Abani had disappeared, and now I only had Adnan to play with.
Look, this is a pistol. A real one. Ready?
Cap gun
I had never seen anything in my life as beautiful as that long, menacing piece of metal.
BANG
A small flame shot out of the end! My ears buzzed. A nice smell wafted under my nostrils.
Come on, let's go shoot someone.
We should find a child to kill. That'll be easier.
We walked for a long time, but we didn't see anyone. So we tried a different floor.
Then Adnan put the pistol close to his ear.
BANG
BEEEP!!! I CAN HEAR: BEEEP!! HA HA HA HA!
God is the greatest! God is the greatest! He is above the plots of the aggressors. And he is the best ally of the oppressed!
With faith and with weapons, I shall defend my country! And the light of truth will shine in my hand!
ADNAN!

BANG!
THWACK
NOOOOO!
CLICK
CLICK
CLICK
MWAAAAAH
I immediately asked my parents for a pistol.
Of course your mother doesn't want you to have one, she's a woman. All boys like weapons. I'll get you one soon.

One of the shows on Libyan TV was a Japanese series called "Specterman." The hero was a robot that defended the earth against the evil schemes of Dr. Gori.
Specterman
The doctor's flying saucer
Dr. Gori was a monkey man who used human pollution to create monsters.
Dr. Gori and his right-hand monkey man
HAHA! So Specterman is being attacked again by the Negroes!
Don't talk like that! It's racist!
Oh, calm down!
What's Negroes?
They're Africans. They're completely black with big thick lips and curly hair...
?!
They look like the bad guys on "Specterman," ha ha...
Dr. Gori is a doctor, remember, just like you...
Pffft, ha!
Mama loves Negroes! Once we were in a nightclub and your mother was sitting on my lap... And a black guy came over, he looked like a gorilla, and he asked your mother to dance!
Can you imagine? If she'd danced with him, I'd have left her then and there, and you'd never have been born!
Thankfully she turned him down...
...
But your mother is right. Some of them are nice.
And intelligent.
LIKE BOKASSA. PFFFT, HEE HEE HEE!

Bokassa is an African dictator who was great friends with Giscard, your mother's president...
He put his opponents in prison, then he roasted them and killed them. And afterward, he ate them... Ha ha!
The cannibal president! Pffft, ha ha!
No, but it's true, you shouldn't say "Negro," especially in France. Because soon there'll be nothing but blacks there. Exactly what the racist Frenchies deserve!
Yet you tried to ask out my West Indian friend before you asked me...
That was a strategic maneuver!
Sometimes, Dr. Gori's right-hand monkey man went about secretly on earth.
He dressed as a human, in classy, manly clothes.
When he did that, I couldn't help thinking...
...that he looked a lot like my father.
What are you staring at?

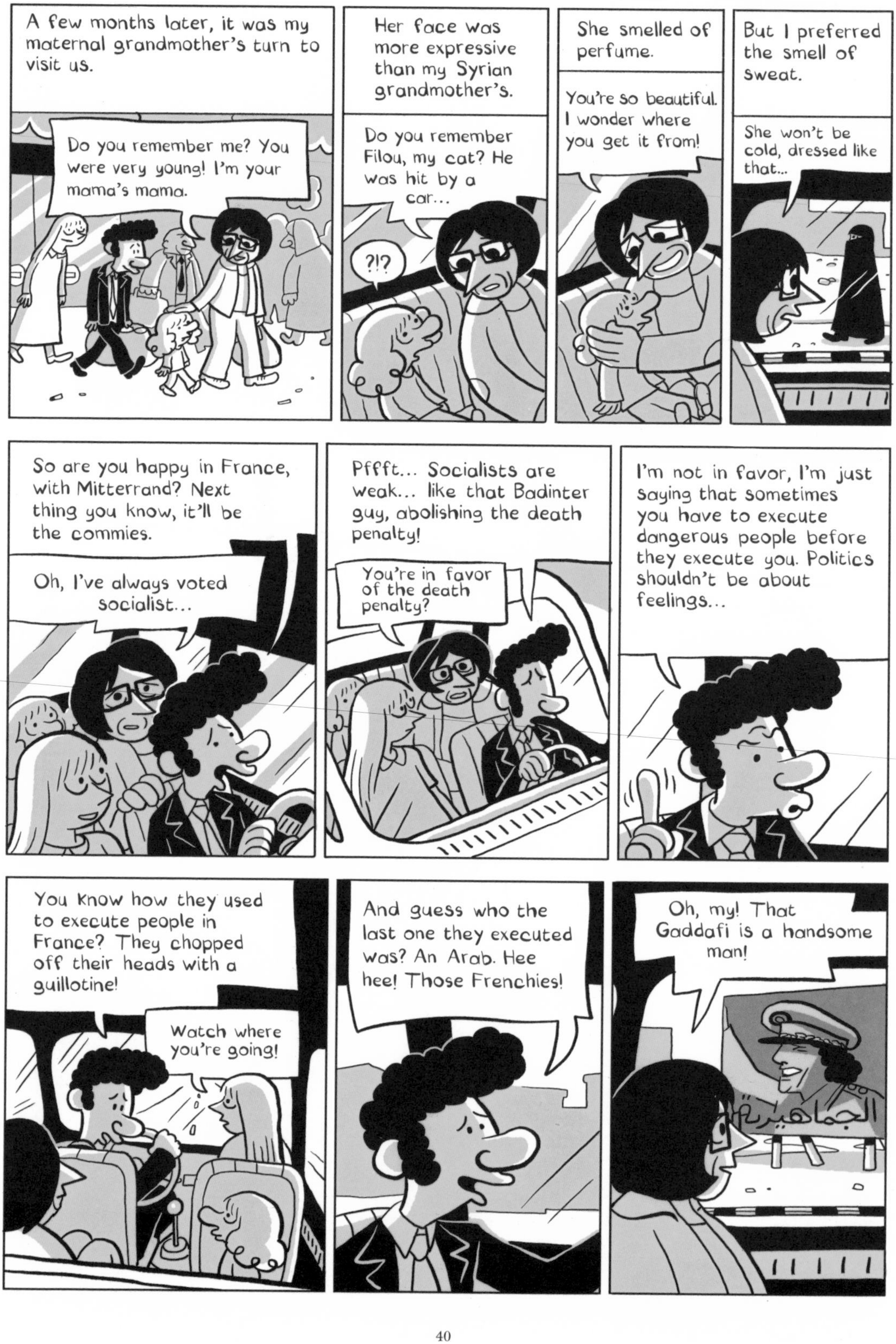
A few months later, it was my maternal grandmother's turn to visit us.
Do you remember me? You were very young! I'm your mama's mama.
Her face was more expressive than my Syrian grandmother's.
Do you remember Filou, my cat? He was hit by a car...
?!?
She smelled of perfume.
You're so beautiful. I wonder where you get it from!
But I preferred the smell of sweat.
She won't be cold, dressed like that...
So are you happy in France, with Mitterrand? Next thing you know, it'll be the commies.
Oh, I've always voted socialist...
Pffft... Socialists are weak... like that Badinter guy, abolishing the death penalty!
You're in favor of the death penalty?
I'm not in favor, I'm just saying that sometimes you have to execute dangerous people before they execute you. Politics shouldn't be about feelings...
You know how they used to execute people in France? They chopped off their heads with a guillotine!
Watch where you're going!
And guess who the last one they executed was? An Arab. Hee hee! Those Frenchies!
Oh, my! That Gaddafi is a handsome man!
الجماهيرية

My grandmother had just divorced my grandfather. She seemed sad. But like everyone else, she admired me.
What are you drawing?
A man.
!
But... that's not just any man, that's... Pompidou!
YOU'RE DRAWING POMPIDOU!
Have you seen his drawing? Incredible!
PRESIDENT POMPIDOU!
He's a genius!
WOW!
Did you know what you were doing? Answer me!
I didn't know who Pompidou was, but the word seemed to impress them all.
I drew POMPIDOU!
...
Unbelievable! Look how he captured his stupid ugly mug!

My mother was happy to see her mother.
Abdel-Razak is going to look for a job in France.
Ohhh! That's great news!
You can't imagine how bored we get here!
He's well paid, but still ...
I got you a subscription to "Paris Match," so that should help.
PARIS MATCH
SARDOU
My father behaved a bit strangely. He kept his suit on the whole day.
So you're going to look for a job in Paris?
Yeah, yeah ...
He left my mother and grandmother chatting on the couch, while he sat on a chair and watched TV.
He seemed to be having an internal conversation with someone.
Can I play with your bull?
Sure, of course!
In fact, he was very worried. He'd talked to his brother in Syria.
Be very careful not to damage it...
He learned that the Syrian army had just destroyed the city of Hama, which was only 25 miles from the family village.
I bought it when I came to France...
There was a Sunni uprising, and 15,000 people had been killed. It hadn't even been mentioned on Radio Monte Carlo.
It's my lucky charm.

On TV, they said that Gaddafi had announced new laws forcing people to swap jobs.
Teachers would now be farmers, and farmers would be teachers. My father was afraid. He talked about leaving Libya earlier than planned.
Would you like to have a little brother to play with?
Huh?
Mama and Papa are going to have another baby like you! You'll be able to play with him.
No, thank you.
But you'll like him, I know you will! The two of you will play soccer together...
It might be a girl, you know...
?!
Ugh, don't jinx it! Not a girl!
I didn't really understand what all this meant, so I decided to pretend that nothing was happening.
I could feel myself growing older. I noticed new things.
For example, the building site outside our window had been abandoned for nearly two years.

And then, one morning in 1982...
I'm taking you to the airport later. Do you want to come with Papa to eat toutes one last time?
CRACK!
Ungh
Say good-bye to the toutes! Say good-bye to the tennis wall!
Good-bye, Libya!
?
Good-bye, Gaddafi!

CHAPTER 2

We landed in France in the middle of the night. My father was staying on in Libya for a few more weeks.

The air in France did not smell the same as in Libya. It was sharper and spicier.

Are you helping him put his little toy together? Shall I do it?

No, it's fine...

He's such a sweetie pie!

A very smiley man came to meet us at the airport. It was my grandfather.

TWA
AIR INTER

I did not remember him at all.

Whoa, you're heavy! Have you been work- ing out?

He had a sour smell and talked about women all the time.

Have you noticed how all the girls look at you?

Let's make the most of it! Here, smile nicely at that pretty girl over there!

Hello

Ooohh! Hey, sweetie!

Ha, he looks like me, don't you think?

I don't know, but I'd happily steal him from you!

Sorry, babe, he's not available, but I am!

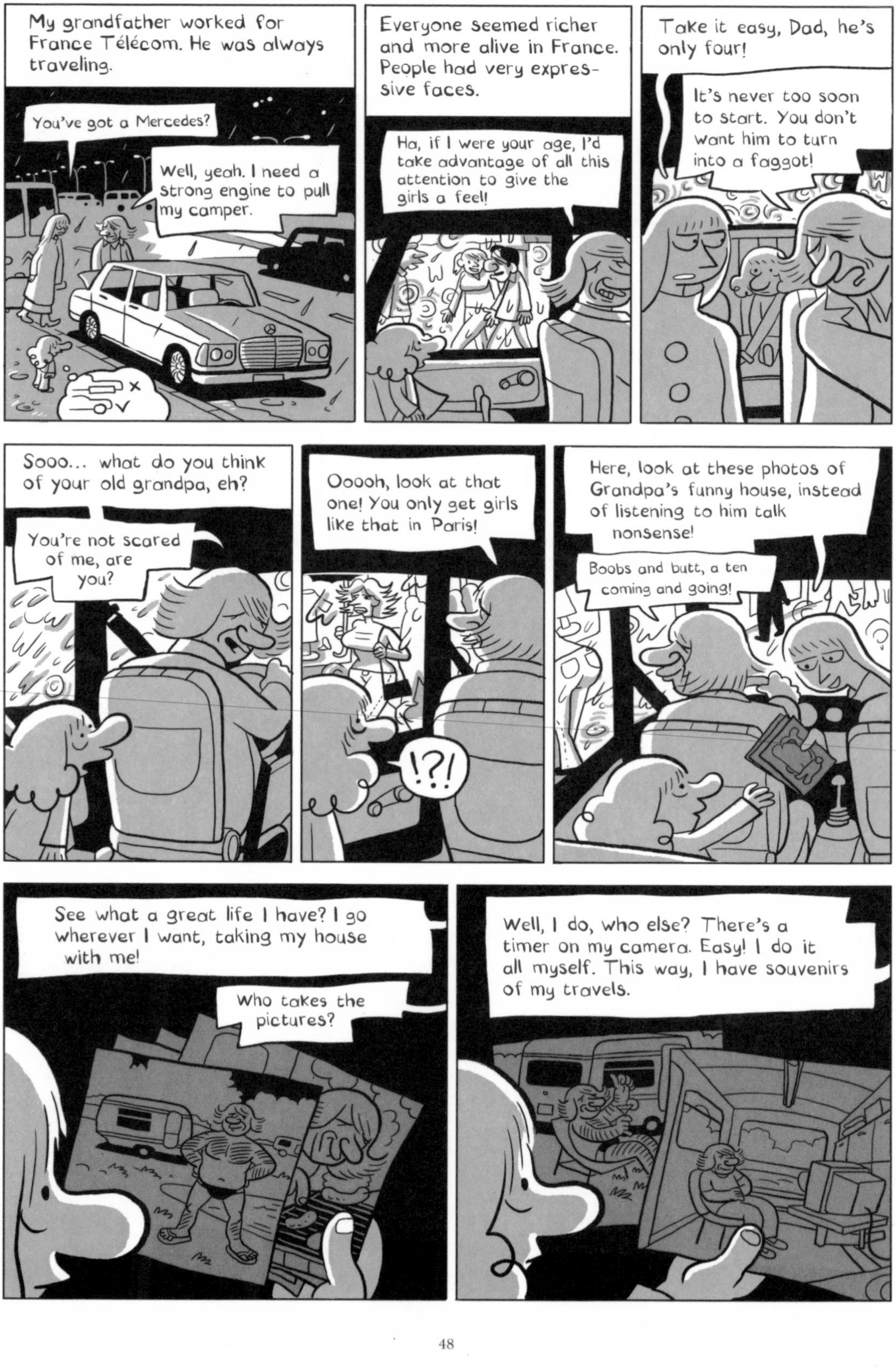

My grandfather worked for France Télécom. He was always traveling.
You've got a Mercedes?
Well, yeah. I need a strong engine to pull my camper.
Everyone seemed richer and more alive in France. People had very expressive faces.
Ha, if I were your age, I'd take advantage of all this attention to give the girls a feel!
Take it easy, Dad, he's only four!
It's never too soon to start. You don't want him to turn into a faggot!
Sooo... what do you think of your old grandpa, eh?
You're not scared of me, are you?
Ooooh, look at that one! You only get girls like that in Paris!
!?!
Here, look at these photos of Grandpa's funny house, instead of listening to him talk nonsense!
Boobs and butt, a ten coming and going!
See what a great life I have? I go wherever I want, taking my house with me!
Who takes the pictures?
Well, I do, who else? There's a timer on my camera. Easy! I do it all myself. This way, I have souvenirs of my travels.

The next day, my grandfather put us on the train to Cap Fréhel in Brittany.
England
LONDON
CAPE FRÉHEL
PARIS
RENNES
France
Atlantic Ocean
BORDEAUX
Spain
And we settled in with my grandmother.
It was an old fisherman's house
...With a large backyard
She lived alone and got pretty bored. She watched TV all day long.
I like Lady Di, she's so pretty.
Yeah, nice house, too. Have you seen it?
My grandmother's home looked like a haunted house.
Upstairs were two large, framed photographs.
My grandma and grandpa.
Granny was a nasty piece of work. When I was your age and I'd come to visit, she'd hit my legs with a stick.
Grandpa was a nice man, but he never said anything. If he had, she'd have hit him, too!
BOOM! BOOM! BOOM!
What's that?
That must be Bébette.

Oh, 'ello! Is he 'ere, lil' Riad?
Yes, he's here. What do you want with him?
She was wearing clogs
Just to see 'im. Ee's so beautiful!
You'll scare him!
Naah, I won't. I'll be very careful, I promise!
He was so small the last time I saw him, with golden hair. He must have grown since then...
OH MY GAWD! He's even more beautiful than before!
Say hello to Bébette.
Hello!
Bébette lived in a tiny house on the other side of the street.
Come wit' me. I'll give you a cookie!
Oh no, don't do that...
Come!
Her house had no water or electricity. She lived in the Middle Ages.
Leave the poor woman alone!
You have to be careful with that one. She's not all there!
Her house smelled of smoke, hay, and earth. The only light came from the fireplace.
Now where did I put the box?
'Ere it is!
Giant eiderdown
Hard earth
Eat 'em nice and slowly, now. You'll stay longer that way!

Ah, I'd have liked to have a lil' one like you . . .
Hee hee hee
He'd have grown up and liked me best . . .
CRUNCH CRUNCH CRUNCH
But now look at me! Lookit' my hands! I never even noticed, I just woke up one mornin' and that's how they were.
Hee hee
CRUNCH CRUNCH GULP
'Ave another cookie! While you're here, I'll pretend you're mine.
Hee hee hee!
CRUNCH CRUNCH CRUNCH GULP CRUNCH CRUNCH CRUNCH CRUNCH
Bébette! It's time for his nap now!
Ha, well, 'course it is!
Bye, lil' Riad! I'm going to bed, too!
THUMP
You have to watch out for Bébette. She seems friendly, but she's completely WACKO!

Then one day I found myself in kindergarten in the village school.
Recess lasted for hours
AARGH!!
Kiss this, kiss this, kiss this.
Ha ha!
I didn't really understand what we were supposed to be doing.
LA LA LI LA LI
I couldn't communicate with the other children at all: a lot of them were unpredictable, always running around in a frenzy.
Hey, you wanna play?
You know, toss the ball around?
WAAAAAAAAH
LOIC, LET GO OF THAT BALL!
NOOOOOO
NEVERRRR
Some of the girls would stand in groups and talk, but without saying anything.
Your dog, he does your dog, he does thaaaaaaat...
Flower, little flower!
Me, well, yeah, me, me
You want to play hide-and-seek?
And your dog your dog, he's got, he's got, he hasn't got, he hasn't got . . .
Little flower, daisy, lazy!!!
Well, yeah.
They seemed really very dizzy, far crazier than even Adnan and Abani had been.
Your dog and your cat and the other cat, they did whaaaat?
?!?

Finally I met a boy who was slightly less crazy than the others. His name was Yaouen.
Let's try to catch each other to see who's fastest!
OK!
GOT YOU! I'M THE BEST!
My dad, he says, he says I'm the best, he says. Your dad, what does he say to you?
My dad, he says that I'm—
Ha ha my dad, if he saw you, he'd say that I'm better than you.
He was completely obsessed with competition.
Look at them ha ha... they suck... they're not fast or good at all...
Nah, we're better than them.
Do you know how to do this?
UNGH!
PFRT
UNG
Ha ha, you can't go as far as me... Look at me, I got this far!
But yeah, okay, we can be friends.
Come on, let's go on the swings. I bet I can go higher than you.
YAOUEN, COME HERE!
I've told you before, you have to tell me when you need to poop!
Look at you! It's disgusting! I'm going to have to tell your father about this!
Waaaa! Waaaah!

We spent almost all our time on creative projects.
My mom she, my mom she...
He doesn't want to...
?
Lalalala
Where did you learn to make animals?
My dad's got one like this! It's on the TV.
Really well proportioned
I was the only one who made recognizable objects.
UNGH!
FLUC
All right, everyone give me your Santa drawings. I'll put them on the wall and we'll look at them together.
WOW
Miiiss
The teacher met with my mother and told her that she wanted to contact the academy about me: my drawings were very advanced for my age.
Maybe he's gifted...
?
Even exceptionally gifted!
REALLY?
He drew a Santa Pompidou...
She thinks he's gifted? I hope not. Kids like that are OK at first, but they often end up retarded.

The next day, I sat next to Yaouen. We were drawing.
You have to . . . ungh . . . do it like that . . . if you want. . . to draw. . . properly. . .
He was completely absorbed in the movement of his pen. And every five seconds, he said a rude word.
Poop!
Pee!
Fart!
I decided to try this, to see how it felt.
UNF
UNF
UNF
UNF
It was amazingly enjoyable to draw meaningless scribble.
Riad? What happened to your nice drawings?
POOP!
Oh, very clever.
HEE HEE HEE
HA HA HA!
Very funny. Enough, every-one, calm down!
HA HA HA
HEE HEE
HA HA
POO-POO
HA HA
After that, I stopped drawing pictures of Pompidou and did the same as everyone else.
Look, I'm the best!
Stop saying that all the time . . .
And no one talked about contacting the academy or me being "exceptionally gifted."
My dad he said that!
And the cat, he haaaaa!
Me!
Bleee

One day, my father reappeared.
He put his briefcase on the table, as usual . . .
CLICK
. . . and took out a magnificent plastic pistol.
It was very exciting to touch things with it.
CLUNK
What a beautiful thing!
That mustache is just silly . . . You'll have to shave it off.
I love my mustache! All the important men have mustaches!
Pfft.
Go on, go, kill your enemies!
Teach them not to mess with Syrians!

My father didn't seem to feel safe in my grandmother's house.
Look at that gate!
It's completely useless!
If someone wants to get in, all they have to do is step over it.
What's the point of having such big trees if you have a little gate like this?
Look, one step and I'm over.
One step and you're over.
The first killer who comes, he'll have no problem at all.
?!?

We often went to Cap Fréhel.
Don't get too close to the edge! Stay in the middle of the path.
All it'd take is a gust of wind and you'd slip and smash your skull on the rocks.
Pffft
We hear the ambulances every day in the summer. They pick up the tourists who died falling off the cliffs.
OH NOOO, I'M GOING TO FALL!
Very funny.
Keep going! One day you'll fall and then you won't be laughing!
When she was young, my mama lived in a house near the edge of the cliffs.
Her father was the lighthouse keeper. The house was ruined but there are still traces of it. I'll show you.
AAAH!

At the end of the spit we saw the old lighthouse and the foundations of a house.
This is where my mother lived when she was young.
Whenever there was a storm, she'd hear the waves hitting the cliffs, and she'd stay awake all night, shaking with fear.
BRRRRRRRRRR
And in the morning, she'd crawl through the ditch for two miles to get to school. She was afraid the wind would blow her away.
WOOOOOOOO
When she got married, she moved to the village.
?
Ungh!
You think we can eat seagulls?
WHAT'S WRONG WITH YOU? OF COURSE NOT!
Too bad...
because they'd be very easy to hunt.

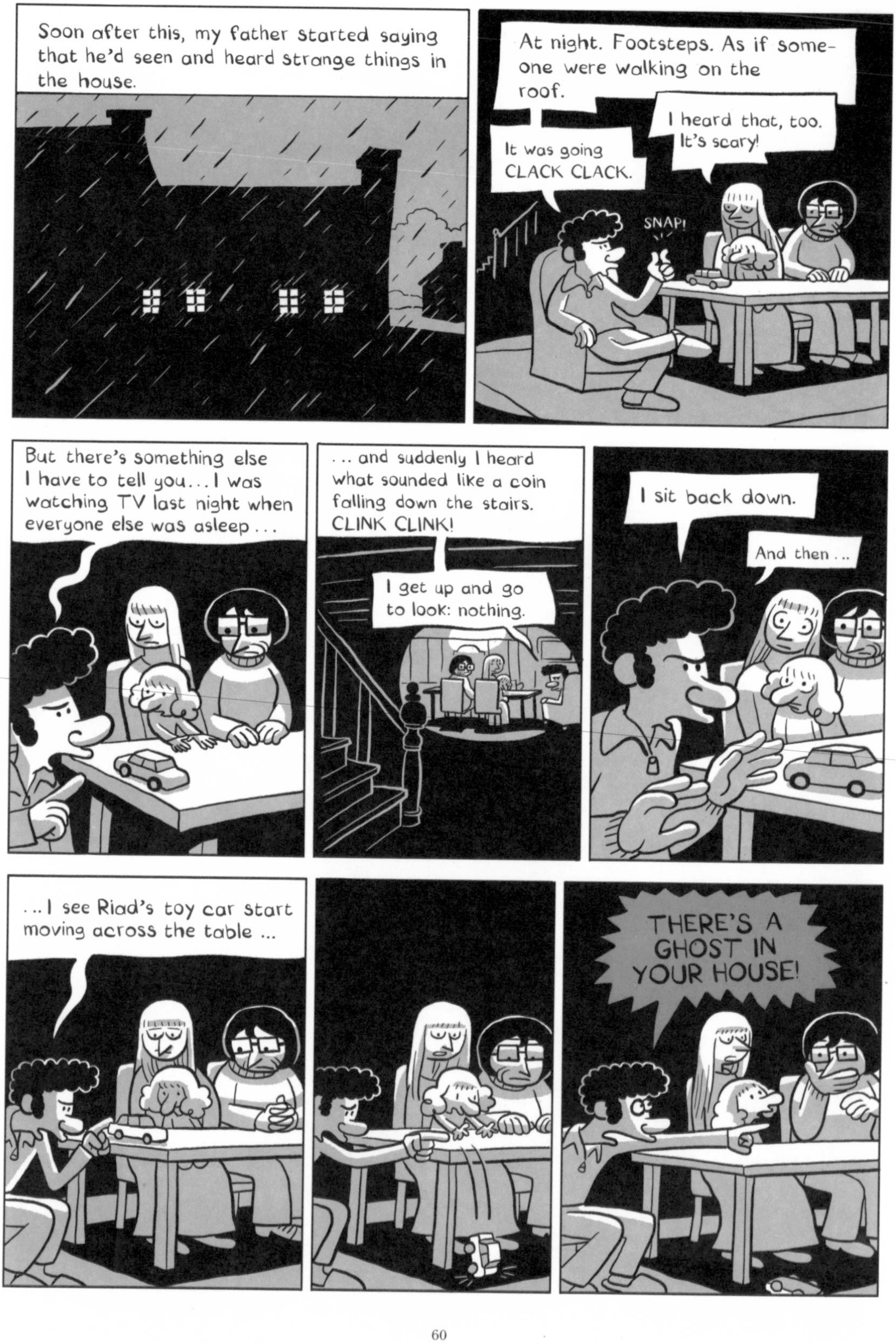

Soon after this, my father started saying that he'd seen and heard strange things in the house.
At night. Footsteps. As if someone were walking on the roof.
It was going CLACK CLACK.
I heard that, too. It's scary!
SNAP!
But there's something else I have to tell you... I was watching TV last night when everyone else was asleep...
... and suddenly I heard what sounded like a coin falling down the stairs. CLINK CLINK!
I get up and go to look: nothing.
I sit back down.
And then...
... I see Riad's toy car start moving across the table ...
THERE'S A GHOST IN YOUR HOUSE!

A few days later, my grandmother took me to the village cemetery
There's someone lying under each of these stones.
What do they do when they get up?
Well, they don't. They stay there forever. They can't move because they're dead.
KR KR
KR
KR
KR
Their soul is with the Lord in heaven.
What's a soul?
It's what leaves the body when you die. It goes to join the Lord in heaven.
KR
KR
KR
And my mother is right here, buried in the ground under this stone.
WHAAT?
Well, yes. That's why I water the flowers.
And my aunt is in this tomb over here. Her name was Mémelle. She died last year.
KR
KR
KR KR KR
Mémelle! If you're the one making noises in the house, you have to stop it: you're scaring everyone.

One morning, I woke up and found myself alone. I called out to my parents: they weren't there.
Good morning! So you're awake? No nightmares, I hope?
I asked where my parents were.
Last night they went to the hospital. Your mama gave birth, you have a little brother.
Isn't that wonderful news?

CHAPTER 3

It turned out my father hadn't been looking for a job in France. Instead, he'd applied to a university in Syria.
Although he'd be one of the most qualified people there, he'd been given the post of assistant professor.
My mother looked tired
All the important positions were given to people with connections.
But we were moving there anyway, to a country where my father said his family had lots of money.
He hadn't been back in 17 years.
I don't like flying. I always think we're going to crash.
Since 1971, Syria had been led by Hafez al-Assad, who had once been a fighter pilot.
Mama, look at my drawing!
"Al Assad" means "the lion." It was not his real name. His real name was "al-Wach," which means "the savage beast."
Syria was a socialist military dictatorship, a close ally of the USSR, and it was at war with Israel.
MAMA, I—
I HEARD YOU! JUST A MINUTE!
Oh what a cute little boy!

The vast majority of the Syrian population was Sunni.
What's his name?
Yahya!
This is the dominant branch of Islam.
Oh, aren't you just gorgeous!
MMFF!
All Muslims believe in the Quran's divine and final authority...
RRFLLNG...
... but Sunnis believe that Mohamed was mankind's last prophet.
RFFL...
My father's family was Sunni.
Pssst!
Shia, the other, minority branch of Islam ...
Hey! You wanna see Pompidou?
... believes that Ali, Mohamed's son-in-law, was the prophet's true successor, and that one day the Mahdi, a messiah, will return.
Mngmng...
Hafez al-Assad was an Alawite, a branch of Shia.
YLHAN ABOUK!
In Syria, the Alawites had been badly persecuted until al-Assad took over the country's leadership.
I had an amazing dream!
After that, he favored his own community, to the detriment of the Sunnis.
I dreamed that the air was full of gold!

Gold, shiny gold, everywhere!
Something magical happened to me when I was your age.
My cousin and I were watching the goats, and we decided to sleep out under the stars.
ZZZ
During the night, I woke up feeling thirsty, so I walked to a spring higher up the mountain. And there I saw the water. It was golden! It shone like gold!
I put my hand in and when it came out it was full of shining gold! It was so beautiful!
I went to wake my cousin, and I showed him the water. We filled our hands with gold and ran to the village to tell the family.
But when we showed them our hands ...
... they were covered with mud! It must have been a curse.
The gold had.. turned to... to mud ...

When we got to the airport in Damascus, the first thing we saw was a gigantic portrait of a man with a mustache and a large forehead: Hafez al-Assad.
The airport was in an even worse state than the one in Libya.
Atini al kbiri!
HEY!
ANA!
As we moved through the corridors, we saw more and more portraits of Assad.
Armed soldiers were checking the passports.
The closer we got to them, the more my father looked worried.
جوازات
Finally, it was our turn.
Ahlan.
Ahlan wasahlan
The soldier looked at the passport, and suddenly stopped.
Khadanit jeshe?
Shu?
A man stared at me.
Slight mischievous grin
It seemed there was something wrong with my father's papers.
Makhadam jeshe? Shahatu al habiss?
Makhadam jeshe!

Iza ma betzabit wad ak mnakhdak halaa ya habib!
Aiwa.
My father asked to speak to the toughest-looking soldier in private.
Hmm
Hmm
Hmm
Strangely, this burly man listened to him carefully, while the other soldiers continued to deal with the line behind us.
Hmm
Ahleen fiik belwatan!
What happened?
Oh, nothing . . . He wanted to check whether I'd done my military service . . .
...since I haven't been back to Syria in 17years...
But I gave him a few dollars, and everything's fine ...
I have nothing to fear, until the next time.
TAXI!
TAXI!
TAXI!

The taxi drivers yelled. It was a screaming contest to get our attention.
TAXI! TAXI! TAXI! TAAAXI! TAXI!
HOMS!
HOMS! HOMS! HOMS! HOMS!
We'll have to wait . . .
Halaa doreyeh!
Laaa! Dorey'ana!
They came to blows.
Etrkhi ya sharmouuut!
Rah! Akhedon anaaa!
After a while, the competition narrowed down to two men.
Men wene gitni intiii?
Rjaa ha dihtak ejarbani!
Ijit a blak!
The losers looked on, smoking and combing their hair.
Finally, the winner, completely out of breath, ushered us into his vehicle.
HUFF
HUFF
HUFF
HOMS
HUFF

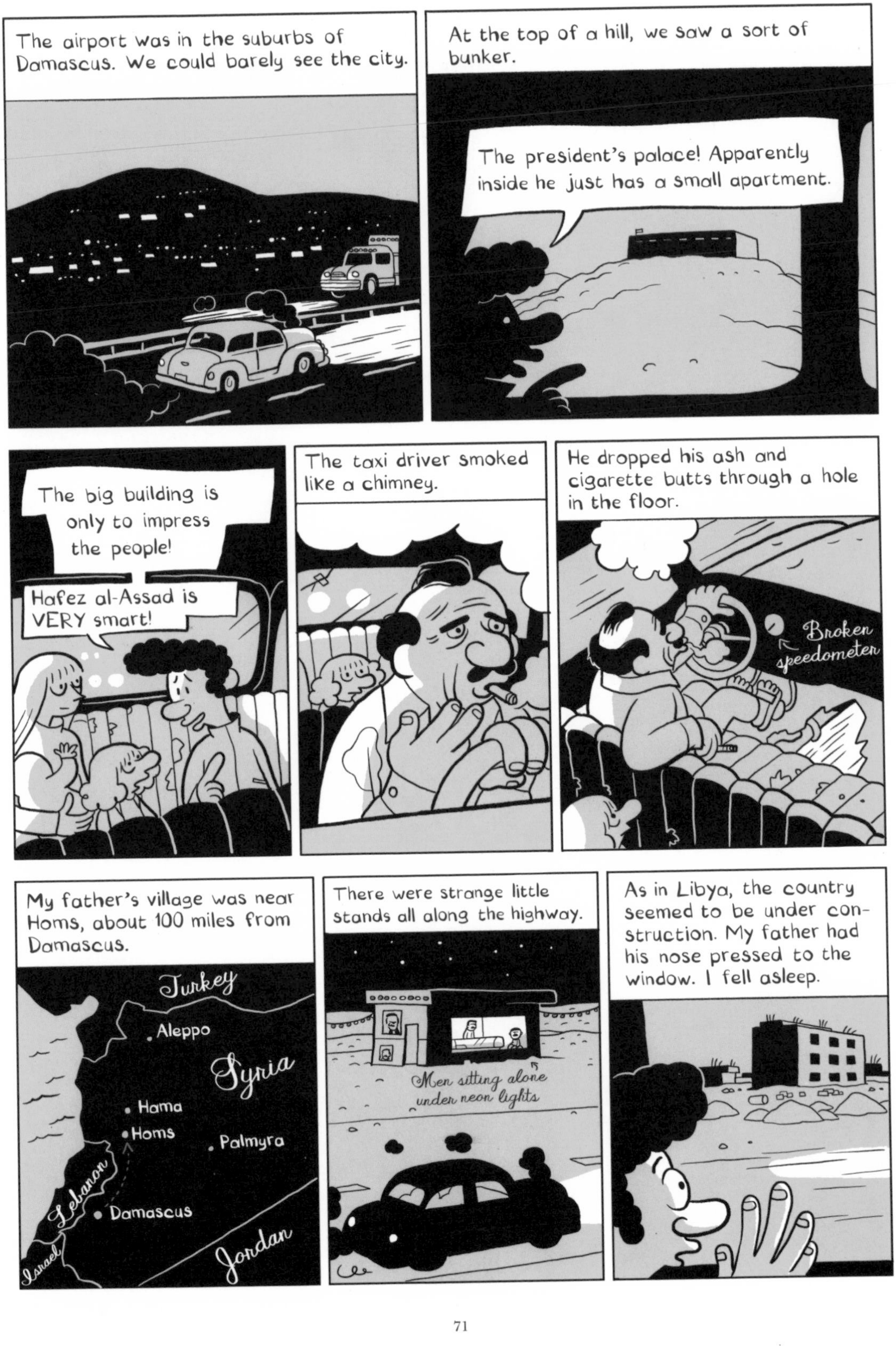

The airport was in the suburbs of Damascus. We could barely see the city.
At the top of a hill, we saw a sort of bunker.
The president's palace! Apparently inside he just has a small apartment.
The big building is only to impress the people!
Hafez al-Assad is VERY smart!
The taxi driver smoked like a chimney.
He dropped his ash and cigarette butts through a hole in the floor.
Broken speedometer
My father's village was near Homs, about 100 miles from Damascus.
Turkey
Aleppo
Syria
Hama
Homs
Palmyra
Lebanon
Damascus
Israel
Jordan
There were strange little stands all along the highway.
Men sitting alone under neon lights
As in Libya, the country seemed to be under construction. My father had his nose pressed to the window. I fell asleep.

When I opened my eyes, we had arrived at my father's village: Ter Maaleh.
We were welcomed by the head of the family, my uncle Haj Mohamed.
My grandmother was there, too. In fact, all the Sattoufs in the village were there.
My uncle welcomed us to his house. At that point, we were separated. My father went into one room with the men...
Tfadali!
See you soon!
...and we went into another, with the women.
Shaaron ashaar he he he!
Garibh!
He he he he
Bishabaho umoun!!
He he.

The women all had their heads covered. The eldest had gold coins under their headdresses.
Ma alazooo
Ma alazooo
Heh heh heh
heh heh heh
Each one had her own particular smell of sweat. Everyone marveled at my blond hair.
Then one of them took off my sock. They all seemed relieved to see my two toes joined together.
My grandmother had the same expression on her face as before, but she looked older.
Li li
Li li
Li li
There were other children in the room. They were whining.
WAAH!
Suddenly, several little boys began to fight.
I'd never seen anything like it: they were pounding each other!
My grandmother urged me to join them.
Rouh elaab, ya Riad!

When I got close to the group, two of the boys pointed at me.
YAHUDI!
?
YAHUDI!
"Yahudi" means "Jew." It was the first word I learned in Syria.
YAHUDI!
YAHUDI!
Gh!
That word provoked great excitement: all the children jumped on top of me.
My mother came to my rescue. I watched the fight from a distance.
Stay here now.
Although I was REALLY hurt, I wanted to get back in the fight. I was drawn, propelled toward the violence.
HUFF!
YAHUUUDI!
YAHUUUDI!

This time, two boys intervened to defend me.
LA! LA! TSSS!
MA YAHUDI!
But one of them managed to tear out a clump of my hair.
RIP!
I hid my head under my mother's sweater.
It's no good crying about it. I told you not to get involved.
Sissy
Quite a long time later, some women brought plates full of rice, bulgur, and gnawed bones.
Using their hands, the women began to eat the remains of the meal eaten by the men in the next room.
Khili! Khili!

After a while, my father reappeared.
Come on, we're done. Let's go!
Sniff
A cousin took us to a house on the other side of the street.
It was gray and looked like it was still being built.
Is this where we'll live?
Sniff
The apartment consisted of one vast, neon-lit entrance hall and four adjoining rooms.
My father lay down on a mattress and began to mumble.
mgmgn
La inti ylhan mngmng
He'd had an argument with his brother, Haj Mohamed.
He's not pleased we're here. He said "You'd be happier in Europe! Why have you come? Go back to France!"
My uncle had sold land belonging to my father and had told him nothing about it.
He's giving us this house in exchange. But it's not worth as much . . .
And he was so nice in Libya!
My own brother!
He sold my land for nothing! And didn't even tell me! He thought I was going to stay in Europe . . .

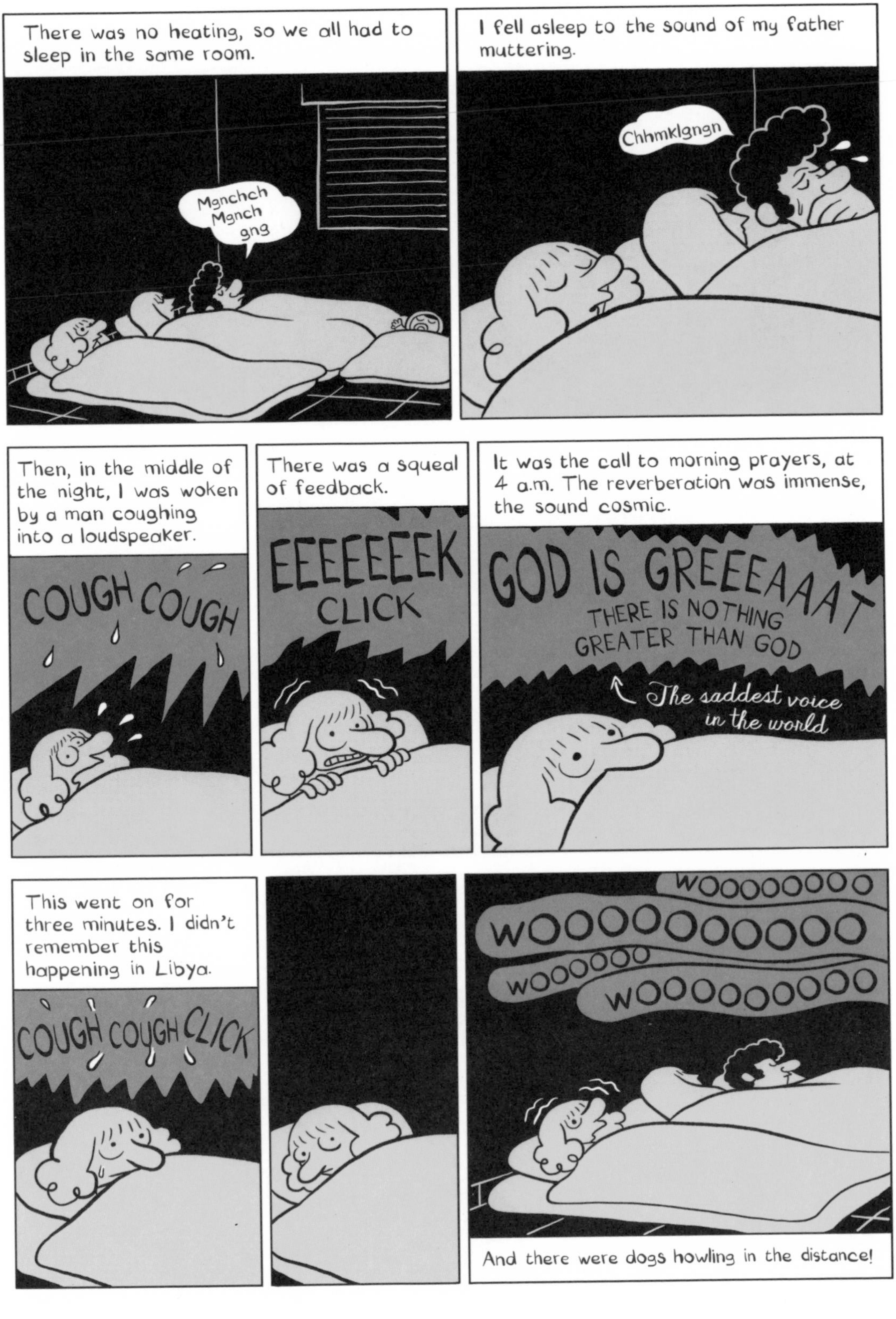

There was no heating, so we all had to sleep in the same room.
Mgnchch Mgnch gng
I fell asleep to the sound of my father muttering.
Chhmklgngn
Then, in the middle of the night, I was woken by a man coughing into a loudspeaker.
COUGH COUGH
There was a squeal of feedback.
EEEEEEEK
CLICK
It was the call to morning prayers, at 4 a.m. The reverberation was immense, the sound cosmic.
GOD IS GREEEAAAT
THERE IS NOTHING GREATER THAN GOD
The saddest voice in the world
This went on for three minutes. I didn't remember this happening in Libya.
COUGH COUGH CLICK
WOOOOOOOOO
WOOOOOOOOOOOO
WOOOOOOO
WOOOOOOOOOO
And there were dogs howling in the distance!

Later that morning, we were woken by yet another call to prayer.
GOD IS GREEEAAAT!
My father wasn't there. I was shivering.
My mother was feeding Yahya.
Hin Khh Hin
It was so cold, my breath steamed.
Ah, you're all awake! Come and look, I've got a surprise!
We could see a flame in the window of the stove.
Look what my sister gave me!
There are olives in this one . . .
. . . and makdous in this one!
Moldy smell
?

My father served breakfast on the floor and sat down. He seemed emotional at the thought of eating Syrian food again.
You'll see— makdous ARE Syria.
Looks like a blood-covered organ
Uh, the bread is still soft. We're going to make it even better.
So we stick the bread on the stove... like this!
Makdous is eggplant with chilis and oil.
Tastes very good
The olives were extremely bitter.
This is inedible!
It's Syrian!
There was also a kind of sheep's cheese soaked in fluorescent yellow oil.
This is the best! You eat a bite with a bit of bread . . .
. . . and take a gulp of very sweet tea . . .
and mix the two up in your mouth.
Then you swallow
GULP
I tried it and it was delicious.
You like that?
YES!
HA! This one's a real Syrian!

After breakfast, we explored the house.
Look! This will make a really nice living room.
This is our bedroom.
This room is for you and your brother.
This room . . . uh, well, let's call it a storeroom!
The kitchen was tiny . . .
. . . and the bathroom enormous.
I had never seen this kind of toilet before. The hole was very deep.
It made me feel a little dizzy.
There was no toilet paper, just a hose.
I could have stayed in that position for hours.

But my mother wasn't too keen on the place.
Look at the walls! They're not painted, and there are cracks everywhere.
That's nothing! It's cracked because it's new! Once it's painted, you won't even see the cracks!
And I don't understand why the entrance hall is the biggest room in the house.
It's so we can organize big receptions with lots of guests!
The tiled floor was perfect for toy cars
We'll go to Homs and buy some luxury furniture...
Don't be mad...
Anyway, it's just temporary. As soon as I can, I'm going to build a beautiful villa on the land I still own.
I'll see an architect next week.
This place is just for a few months.
We'll have a huge garden filled with fruit trees, and a magnificent driveway leading to the house.
All the people in Ter Maaleh will be jealous, ha ha ... And I'll drive home in my brand-new Mercedes ...
And I'll drive very slowly up the driveway, to savor the sweetness.

We went up onto the roof to take in our surroundings. The village was quite small and all the houses looked the same.
See how pretty it is?
They were all gray and looked unfinished. Long bits of metal poked up from the other roofs, just like ours.
In Syria, you only have to pay taxes on the house when it's finished. Nobody wants to pay, so they never finish their houses!
HA HA!
We could also see a sort of old town made of earth, which seemed to be in ruins.
Anyway, who cares what the outside looks like? When it's so beautiful inside . . .
It was a very windy place. Plastic bags were constantly flying across the sky.
To the north, the horizon was flat, except for one huge hill.
To the east, it was flat except for two small hills.

To the west, a rocky outcrop: the Djebel Asariyeh.
There were Alawite villages there
To the south, an enormous mountain stood out against the sky: the Qurnat as-Sawda', the highest peak of Mount Lebanon.
Totally biblical
We could also make out Homs and its refinery, which burned night and day.
Can you see the space between those two houses? Well, there's treasure buried there!
It's from Roman times.
One day, I'm going to buy a metal detector!
That's a machine that tells you if there's gold in the earth.
I'll go there one night, without telling anyone . . .
I'll find the gold and I'll be a multibillionaire.

We went to visit the village.
A road ran in front of the house.
Ha ha! Syrians drive like real men!
HOOOOONNNK
TOYOTA
All these new houses, it's crazy! I want to show you where I lived when I was young.
The streets were littered with plastic bags and trash that looked as if it had been there a long time.
In spite of the cold, a faint smell of shit floated in the air.
People's dogs poop in the street here, just like in France! HA HA!
NOOOOO!
People don't have dogs here! What a horrible idea!
In France, people with dogs are the dogs of their dogs!
So what is it, then?
Um, that's just how things are. Don't look at it.

So this is where I lived with my brothers and sisters . . .
That was when I was very young.
I like the stones. Buildings used to be more solid.
Yeah! When I build my luxury villa, I'll have stones just like these put above the door. It'll look amazing!
This is the old abandoned village.
People lived here for thousands of years before Christ.
Wild onions growing through the walls
But be careful! There are genies roaming these alleys . . .
Genies are the friends of Satan!
Satan is evil! Let me tell you what happened to my uncle here, a long time ago . . .
WHOA!

Imchi ya walad!
WAAAAAH!
So it's the children!
People are poor . . . What else can you do if you're a kid and you need to go out in the street?
Anyway, I was about to tell you what happened to my uncle here, years ago . . .
One night, after spending the day in the fields with his goats, he brought them back to the pen. But there was a problem, they didn't want to go inside.
?!?
He hit them, but it did no good. Suddenly, he heard a voice in the night . . .
Don't strike them. They are afraid of me.
My uncle jumped. There was an old woman in the goat pen.
What are you doing here, old woman? Get out! This pen is for my goats.
I am an old beg-gar with nowhere to go . . . Please let me sleep here tonight . . .
My uncle, who was very devout, let her stay out of charity.
GET IN THERE, YOU STUPID ANIMAL!
Wait . . . Let me help you . . .
MEH

Come on, little ones, fear not. Come inside.
Agggh!
Meh!
Meh!
The woman was a genie, working her magic.
He pissed his djellaba and ran away!
MEEEEH!
HUH!
MEEEEH!
?
HUMPH!
Son of a dog!
MEH!
Why did you do that?
HA HA! Look at that butt face!
Sometimes, Satan hides himself inside an animal!
What's Satan?
He's the enemy of God!
?!
?
The people stared at us as if we were extraterrestrials.

Ter Maaleh was a Sunni village. My mother was the only European in the area.
So, that's the first river ...
There were two rivers. The first one was called Saquiieh. It was black and looked like a sewer.
Come back! Don't get too close ...
Smell of shit
I used to swim in there when I was young!
The water was clean then.
The second river was further down and looked more impressive. It was the Oronte.
It's full of moorhens down there!
One night, I laid a trap to catch one. I came back in the morning, and I could see crows circling above the place where I'd left my trap.
It was too late. Those bastards had eaten my moorhen!
Crows are cunning. They watch you from the corners of their eyes, and when you leave, they steal your things!
We were being followed by the boy who pooped in the street

Until the First World War, Syria had been part of the Ottoman Empire. As Turkey chose to ally itself with Germany, its empire was carved up after the defeat.
This pump hasn't changed!
Gni
France was given a mandate over Syria, which lasted from 1920 to 1943.
The entire irrigation system was built by the French. It's still in use.
I played here when I was young. And we swam there.
Be careful, though. Kids have drowned in this reservoir.
Suddenly, amid the garbage, I saw something wriggle.
See them? Their heads make them look like snakes.
They're turtles! Little turtles!
Follow us!
Zairtertelz! Leeltertelz!
Perfect imitation of a posh accent
Pfft.

We looked for moorhens but didn't find any.
The current was strong
Mama, there's mosquitoes!
MAMMAZAIRZMOSKEETOOHHZ
HAHA
Even better imitation
Three of them were behind us now.
ZAIRZ MOSKEET OOHHZ!
Never mind. Just ignore them!
Ha ha!
Hang on, I think I've got a stone in my shoe.
BOO
HISS
YAHUDI!
The children behind us looked pretty threatening. They tried to look tough and banged their sticks on the ground.
HISS
YAHUDI!
GRRR
So, do you like it here?
Yes. It's polluted, though.
YAHUDI!
HISS!

He was all over them in the blink of an eye. The children tried to outrun him . . .

. . . but he was too fast.

Seeing those kids who had teased me get beaten gave me great pleasure.

I was thrilled by the sight of their faces twisted in pain and misery . . .

. . . but after a while, I began to feel something strange.

Next, my father took us to the other side of the village, where he showed us the only field that still belonged to him after his brother had sold all the others.
Sniff
This is where I'll build my luxury villa. It's a good spot, don't you think?
?
Land is everything, it's more important than money! Nothing bad can happen to you when you have your own land.
Before, all this was mine. All these fields . . .
We walked until we came to a huge tree by the side of the road.
Your great-grandfather planted this. It's the biggest toute tree in the village.
There's a power cable going through the branches: watch out you don't electrocute yourself if you ever climb up the tree!
?!?

The power cables were connected to a house that was unique in this village: it had a tiled roof that looked finished.
In fact, it wasn't
U.N. AID
It belongs to my cousin Mohamed, a general...
YOU HAVE A COUSIN WHO'S A GENERAL?
Well, we're pretty much cousins with the whole village...
BVV
There are lots of generals in Syria, anyway. Since they all have the same rank, they're suspicious of one another. That way, they won't attempt a coup.
Suddenly, a Jeep roared away from the house.
VRROOOM
HOONNNK
U.N. AID
HOONNNK
VRRROOM
Quick, out of the way.
Now!
HOONNK
HOONNK
The driver is just a kid!
Probably the general's son!
VRROOM

We went to see the village school.
This is where I learned to read and write.
It hasn't changed a bit!
The school was too small to have all the children there at the same time.
You'll be going soon!
Gni
So the students took turns: some went three mornings a row, some three afternoons.
Apparently they're building a bigger one with room for everyone.
In my day, nobody went to school. Parents didn't believe in sending their children.
Like with me, I'm the only one of my brothers and sisters who can read. They let me go because I was the youngest.
See that flag? I stole it one night with a friend, because we liked the colors—the red and the green!
We replaced it with a dirty old rag, and the next day we went to school as if nothing had happened.

But what we'd done was very serious. They gathered all the students in the playground and asked, "Who stole the flag of the glorious Syrian nation?"
Nobody answered. So the teacher said, "If you know the culprit and you denounce them, I will give you five Syrian pounds."
So my friend, who was stupid, put his hand up and said, "It was us, sir! Can we have the five pounds?"
HA HA HA HA HA HA! He REALLY believed they'd give him the five pounds!
HA HA! They grabbed us and said we were going to be publicly executed, as an example to the others!
Ha ha
A man went to fetch a rifle, and we thought we were going to die. We were crying! We were crying! Ha ha!
But in fact they just fetched a stick and hit us with it so hard that we couldn't sit down for the next week!
As we were leaving, I saw a student in uniform running toward the water fountains.
He drank, with his mouth touching the hole.
Then he took a piss, aiming at the hole.

We went back to see my grandmother.
She lived in my uncle's house, on the other side of the street
My father lay in her lap, just as in Libya.
Then he began to talk to her, exaggerating his expressions.
Emmii, aliloy yrajaali almassaarii!
Uh huh.
It sounded like he was complaining.
Hedol massaryeh. . .
There, there.
Suddenly, two children came into the room, the same two who had attacked me the previous evening.
Tahal! Tahal!
Their names were
Anas
&
Moktar
My father sat up and stopped his complaining.
KISS KISS
Heh! Heh!
My uncle Haj Mohamed entered the room and greeted us all as if everything were fine.
MWAH MWAH

Anas and Moktar started whining.
There was something in my eye
Waaaah
My uncle clicked his tongue very loudly.
CLACK!
The two children sat against the wall in silence.
I realized that Anas and Moktar were Haj Mohamed's children.
Those two brutes were my cousins.
Ting!
Everyone was smiling, but it was obvious that my father and my uncle hated each other.
Go pick up the coin. He's giving it to you.
Li li li li!
HA HA!

Gradually, the whole family assembled in my grandmother's room.
Haj Mohamed had two wives. The first was elderly and sometimes talked to herself.
She was extremely sweet and kind, but didn't seem quite all there
Ma fi mgnmgn
The second one was younger. She was Anas and Moktar's mother.
Yep, definitely their mother
After a while, my uncle left the room.
Stop rubbing. It'll get infected and you'll lose your eye . . .
Your grandmother has a magical way to get dirt out of eyes.
She's going to lick your eyeball!
Um, she's not really going to do that, is she?
Of course! You'll see . . .
Here, here . . .

My grandmother gripped my head in her hands.
People were giggling. I could feel her rough tongue under my eyelid.
Finally, she stood me on my feet.
My eye didn't hurt anymore!
Moktar and Anas ran toward her . . .
Waaah!
Waaah!
. . . and she licked their eyeballs, too, so they wouldn't be jealous.

My father went to Damascus once a week to teach.
My mother stayed in bed, looking after my little brother
Vrrrrroooom
Goo goo D D
I wasn't allowed outside because I was too little, so I looked through the window.
The woman across the street hung out her laundry even when it was raining. She put her baby on the concrete floor.
When she finished, she picked him up by one leg.
Wah Wah
And once he'd gotten a tight grip on her, she covered him with kisses.
From the kitchen balcony, I could see another house.

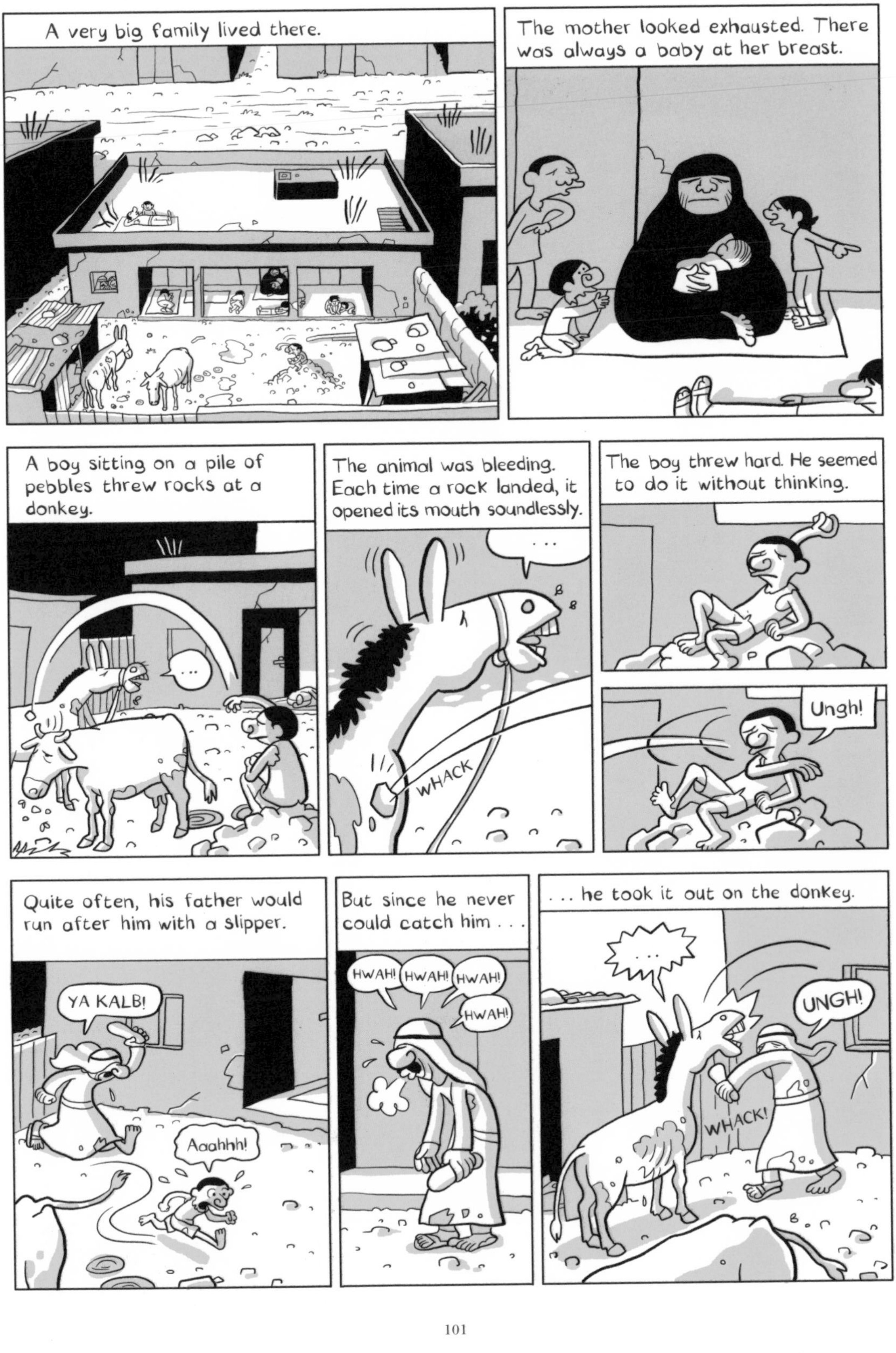
A very big family lived there.
The mother looked exhausted. There was always a baby at her breast.
A boy sitting on a pile of pebbles threw rocks at a donkey.
. . .
The animal was bleeding. Each time a rock landed, it opened its mouth soundlessly.
. . .
WHACK
The boy threw hard. He seemed to do it without thinking.
Ungh!
Quite often, his father would run after him with a slipper.
YA KALB!
Aaahhh!
But since he never could catch him . . .
HWAH!
HWAH!
HWAH!
HWAH!
. . . he took it out on the donkey.
. . .
UNGH!
WHACK!

I spent hours watching the main street and the water tower.
At noon, the school kids would run home . . .
. . . then reappear in the afternoon, armed to the teeth.
With great accuracy, they shot pebbles at the streetlights, even though they were already smashed to pieces.
Now and then, two gangs would square off. The boys would strike thuggish, threatening poses.
But it rarely degenerated into an actual fight: they were all cousins.
I dreamed of going out to join them. They looked so tough.
In the evening, my father would come home from university.

He seemed more worried than he'd been in Libya. He would quickly take off his suit, as if he were afraid of being seen in it.
He would put on a djellaba, sit on the floor, and smoke a cigarette.
So, what did you do today?
I played!
Again? Aren't you bored of just playing all the time?
Wouldn't you prefer to go to school with friends?
No, I want to stay with Mama.
"Wah wah I want to stay home with Mama"... You can't stay with your mother all your life, you know.
I went to school when I was your age.
You can't send him to school. He doesn't even speak Arabic!
Pffft. He'd learn it in two days... I think he should go. It'll toughen him up...
Instead of staying in the house all day, playing with little cars and naked plastic men...
Whooosh
I liked being at school when I was a kid. I was happier there than at home...

The days passed in the apartment. My father no longer talked about his luxury villa.
My mother looked increasingly tired
Vrroom, no you vrroom
Ga ga
Hey, Riad, come meet some new friends.
These are your cousins Mohamed and Wael. Mohamed is a year older than you, and Wael is your age.
Ahahaha
Mohamed
Combed hair
Wael
Neatly dressed
I remembered them: they had defended me in that fight on my first evening.
Shall we go and play?
Speaking French
??!
BWAHAHAHA
SHALWEGOANPLEY?
HEE HEE HEE HEE
In Syria the custom was to take your shoes off before going indoors.
!
Their shoes were plastic moldings of real sneakers!
Even the knot in the laces was molded!
An odd color!
Left and right were identical!

They were completely fascinated by my toys.
!!!
?!?
Shouf the Sihara! Shouf like so cool!
I was beginning to understand a few words
They carefully looked at each one, as if it were an object of great value.
Ha! Wow!
They greatly admired the mechanical systems that allowed the car doors to open and could bend the action figures' elbows.
?
They were determined to find out what was inside each toy.
They were extremely thorough. They did things I'd never even thought of doing.
Arranging the cars in a straight line! What a brilliant idea!
We played for a while. Then my father came to tell them it was time for them to leave.
The nicest guys in the world
It turned out we were neighbors. We lived on the same floor.

There was nothing to do in Ter Maaleh: no cafés, no restaurants, no shops. Nothing but houses and families.
Occasionally we'd go shopping in Homs, about four and a half miles away.
An old bus made the trip every hour.
He put the coin in his pocket
We could see the road rush under us through the floor.
People kept staring at us.
By the side of the road, we saw a huge sugar refinery, half-destroyed ...
With Bedouin tents in front
... then some newer-looking grain silos.
This was a forest when I was young. Now it's the modern world.

As we got closer to Homs, we saw more and more posters of Hafez al-Assad.
There were large painted billboards where he looked younger.
There was a statue of him in the middle of a traffic circle.
Sculpted tie
Every available space was covered with posters and stickers.
I noticed then that the bus was full of them, too.
With his mustache, even the bus driver looked like Assad.
Chair fixed with nails
In fact, every man on the bus had a mustache, except for my father.
I didn't like Assad as much as Gaddafi. He wasn't as handsome or sporty. He had a large forehead, and there was something shifty-looking about him. You couldn't really see his eyes.

The first time I went to Homs, it was raining.
Everywhere you looked, there were chicks for sale.
One guy lifted up one of the plastic cages. He picked up a lifeless chick . . .
. . . and tossed it onto a big pile of other lifeless chicks.
All the cars were honking their horns and all the people were shouting. There was garbage everywhere and it stank.
HONNKK
HONKKK
HONNKKK
Oops!
The buildings looked like they were about to collapse, and they were black with dirt.
Who could possibly stand on these balconies?
My father took us to a souk.
Look at the lights!

We saw a guy who sold nothing but plastic bowls. He was very polite and kind to us.
He offered me a bucket
It was likely fear that made him so obliging: my mother was European, so he thought my father might be in the regime.
Do you know him?
Nope, not at all.
We went to the kebab stalls in search of something to eat.
You have to use your nose to find the best one.
Most of the restaurants gave off a bitter, rancid smell.
Li li li!
The ground was covered with old food. Rats ran all over the place.
Look at that filthy bastard!
HA HA HA!
Eeek
Men ate standing in the street, none of them talking.
Wow, the prices have really gone up! Bunch of thieves!
We walked past a stall where my uncle Haj Mohamed was sitting at a table.
My father pretended not to notice, but my uncle had seen us. He waved at me with his sandwich.

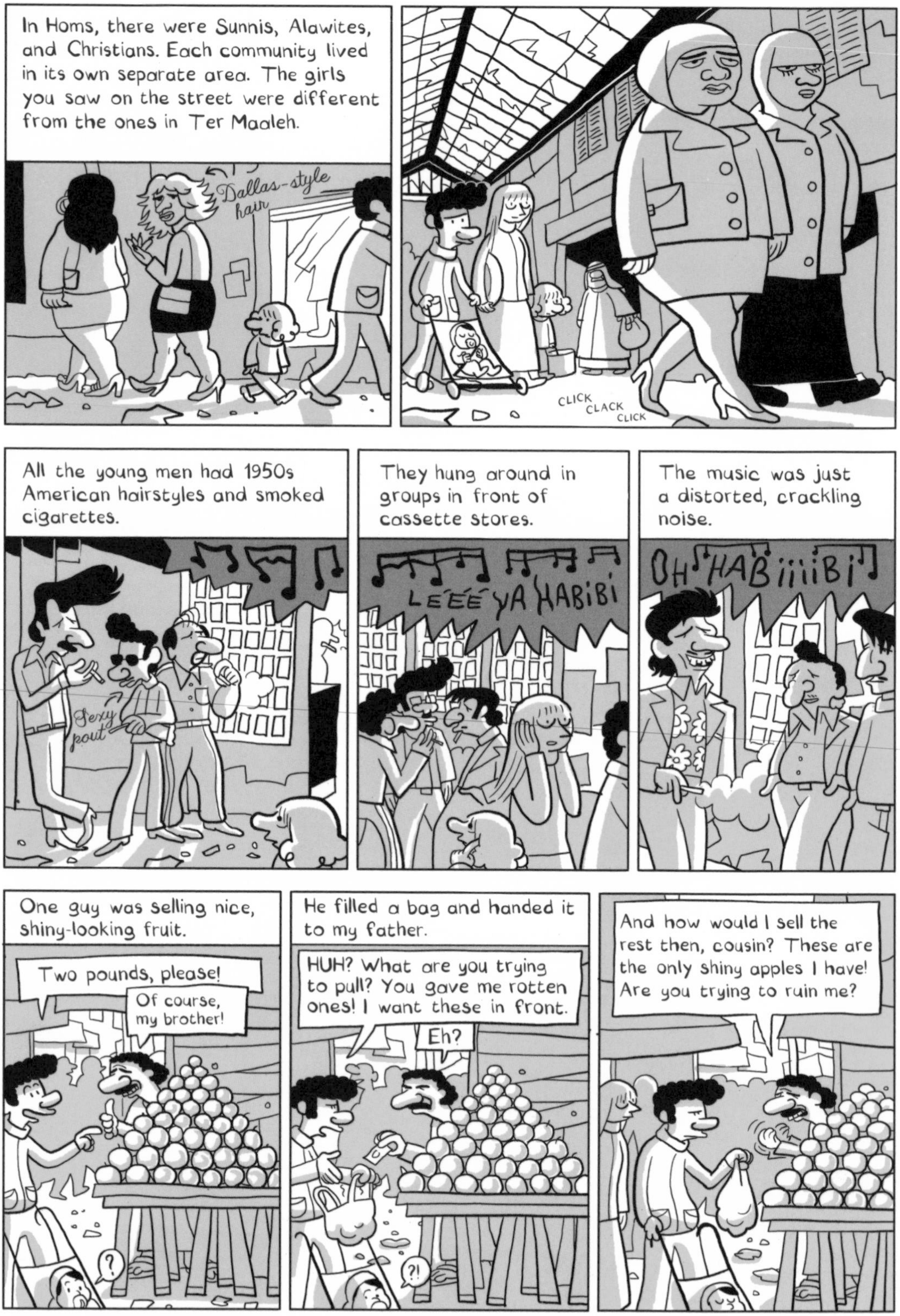
In Homs, there were Sunnis, Alawites, and Christians. Each community lived in its own separate area. The girls you saw on the street were different from the ones in Ter Maaleh.
Dallas-style hair
CLICK CLACK CLICK
All the young men had 1950s American hairstyles and smoked cigarettes.
Sexy pout
They hung around in groups in front of cassette stores.
LEÉÉ YA HABIBI
The music was just a distorted, crackling noise.
OH HABiiiiBi
One guy was selling nice, shiny-looking fruit.
Two pounds, please!
Of course, my brother!
?
He filled a bag and handed it to my father.
HUH? What are you trying to pull? You gave me rotten ones! I want these in front.
Eh?
?!
And how would I sell the rest then, cousin? These are the only shiny apples I have! Are you trying to ruin me?

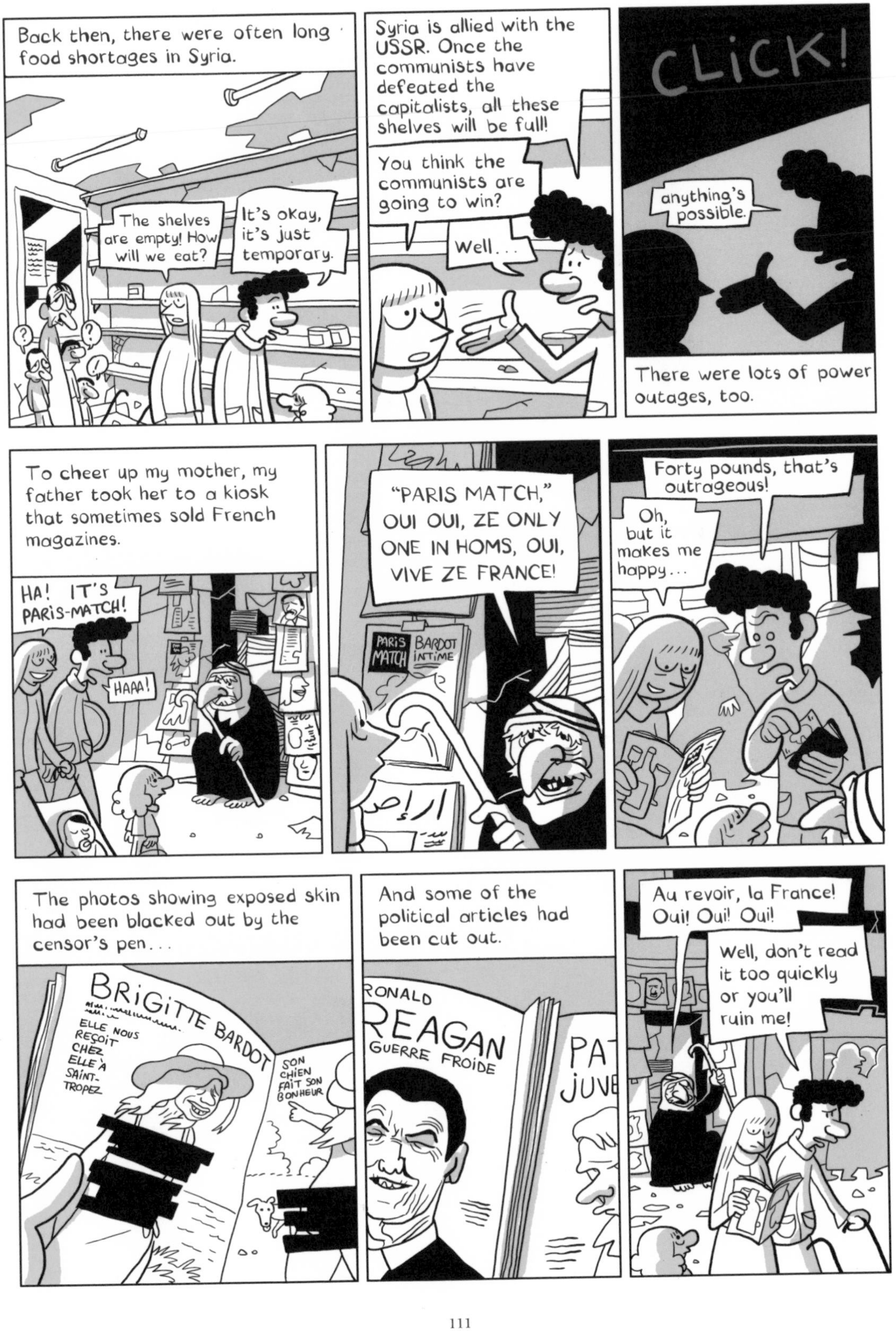

Back then, there were often long food shortages in Syria.
The shelves are empty! How will we eat?
It's okay, it's just temporary.
Syria is allied with the USSR. Once the communists have defeated the capitalists, all these shelves will be full!
You think the communists are going to win?
Well...
CLICK!
anything's possible.
There were lots of power outages, too.
To cheer up my mother, my father took her to a kiosk that sometimes sold French magazines.
HA! IT'S PARIS-MATCH!
HAAA!
"PARIS MATCH," OUI OUI, ZE ONLY ONE IN HOMS, OUI, VIVE ZE FRANCE!
PARIS MATCH
BARDOT INTIME
Forty pounds, that's outrageous!
Oh, but it makes me happy...
The photos showing exposed skin had been blacked out by the censor's pen...
BRIGITTE BARDOT
ELLE NOUS REÇOIT CHEZ ELLE À SAINT-TROPEZ
SON CHIEN FAIT SON BONHEUR
And some of the political articles had been cut out.
RONALD REAGAN
GUERRE FROIDE
PAT
JUVE
Au revoir, la France! Oui! Oui! Oui!
Well, don't read it too quickly or you'll ruin me!

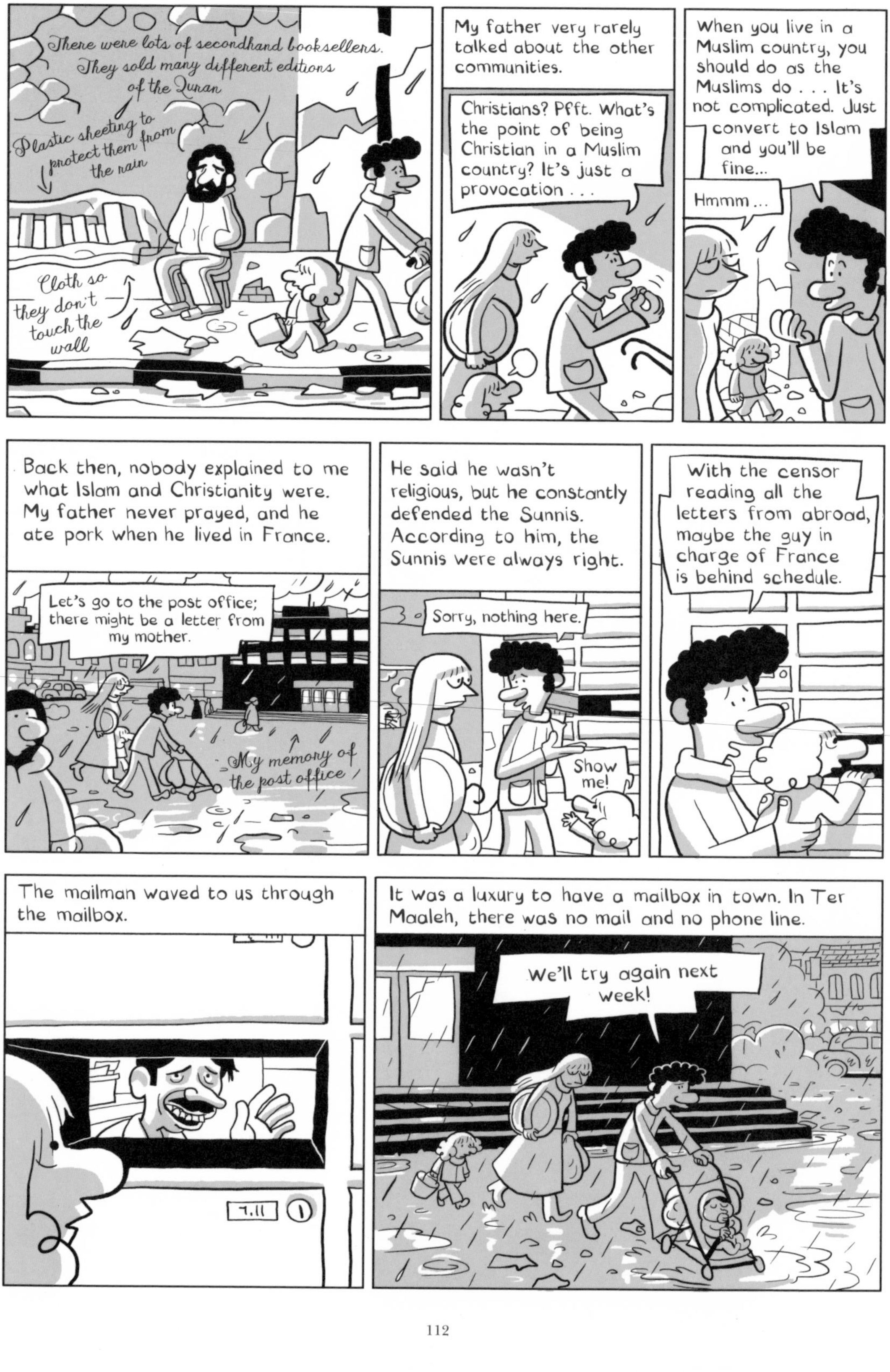
There were lots of secondhand booksellers. They sold many different editions of the Quran
Plastic sheeting to protect them from the rain
Cloth so they don't touch the wall
My father very rarely talked about the other communities.
Christians? Pfft. What's the point of being Christian in a Muslim country? It's just a provocation . . .
When you live in a Muslim country, you should do as the Muslims do . . . It's not complicated. Just convert to Islam and you'll be fine...
Hmmm...
Back then, nobody explained to me what Islam and Christianity were. My father never prayed, and he ate pork when he lived in France.
Let's go to the post office; there might be a letter from my mother.
My memory of the post office
He said he wasn't religious, but he constantly defended the Sunnis. According to him, the Sunnis were always right.
Sorry, nothing here.
Show me!
With the censor reading all the letters from abroad, maybe the guy in charge of France is behind schedule.
The mailman waved to us through the mailbox.
It was a luxury to have a mailbox in town. In Ter Maaleh, there was no mail and no phone line.
We'll try again next week!

KERBOOOOM!
What is that? AGH,
IT'S HORRIBLE!
Oops!
They just leave them hanging like that?
That's life!
It's horrible, but it's necessary. It sets an example. This way, people stay peaceful and law-abiding. You have to frighten them . . .

On the bus ride home, my father bumped into an old childhood friend.
ABU RIAD!
TAMER
They were happy to see each other. They seemed to really like each other.
Abu Riad . . . Kiff is it going?
Tamer, my old friend!
Tamer called my father "Abu Riad," father of Riad.
And this is Riad!
Li li li!
At a certain age, men can choose to be addressed by the name of their future son. My father chose my name years before he met my mother.
Riad! Betaaref awal sura?
Tamer began asking me questions but I didn't understand what he was saying....
Yallah! Jareb! Jareb tqolha!
What's he asking him?
Pfft. He wants to know if Riad has memorized the first sura of the Quran.
Manak hafezha?
Mani messadak!
Lazem tkoon hafezha aah ghaieb!
Ha ha
SSSSSSSSS!
AAAHH!

SSSSSSSS!
AAHHH! AAAAAH HHH!
SSSSSSSSSSSS!
AAAHH! AAAAHHH!
As my father imitated a snake, Tamer curled up in a ball.
HA! HA! HA!
Sniff. Sniff. Sniff.
SSSS!
AAAAAHH!
SSSSSS!
Boo hoo
Boo hoo
HAHA
HAHA
HAHA
Tamer began to cry loudly.
Waah, waah, waah!
My father gave him a hug to console him.
HA HA, he's so afraid of snakes, they make him cry! HA HA!
When we were young, his parents sent him to school. They were very poor...
He was very good at school, but one day someone found out he was scared of snakes! After that, everyone used to hiss at him... He couldn't stand it...
So he quit school because of that! HA HA HA HA! THE WUSS!

Later that evening . . .
Riad, come, there's something I want to read to you.
?
Look, it's the Quran. This book is holy for all of us Muslims.
?
The archangel Gabriel dictated it to the Prophet. I'm going to read you the first sura. Listen.
He began reading, showing me the words with his finger as he went. The look on his face was not the same as usual. This seemed to be extremely important.
Of course, I understood none of it. But the sounds of the words were beautiful and mesmerizing.
So you like it?
Uh, sure!
So now it's your turn to read. You have to learn this by heart!
GO ON!
READ!
? ! ? ? ? ! ! ?
HA HA HA HA HA HA!
I'M KIDDING! YOU DON'T KNOW HOW TO READ!
HA HA!

To read the Quran, you have to know how to read. Right?
Well, yes!
So good! You'll be starting school next week.
School is mandatory. Everyone goes to school. So you'll do the same.
But I can't speak! I can't understand what anyone's saying!
You DO understand!
You spoke Arabic very well in Libya!
You're just saying it so you don't have to go to school!
ADMIT IT!
I'm against it. He's still so little and—
HE'S OLD ENOUGH, PERIOD!
I'm the one who makes the decisions!

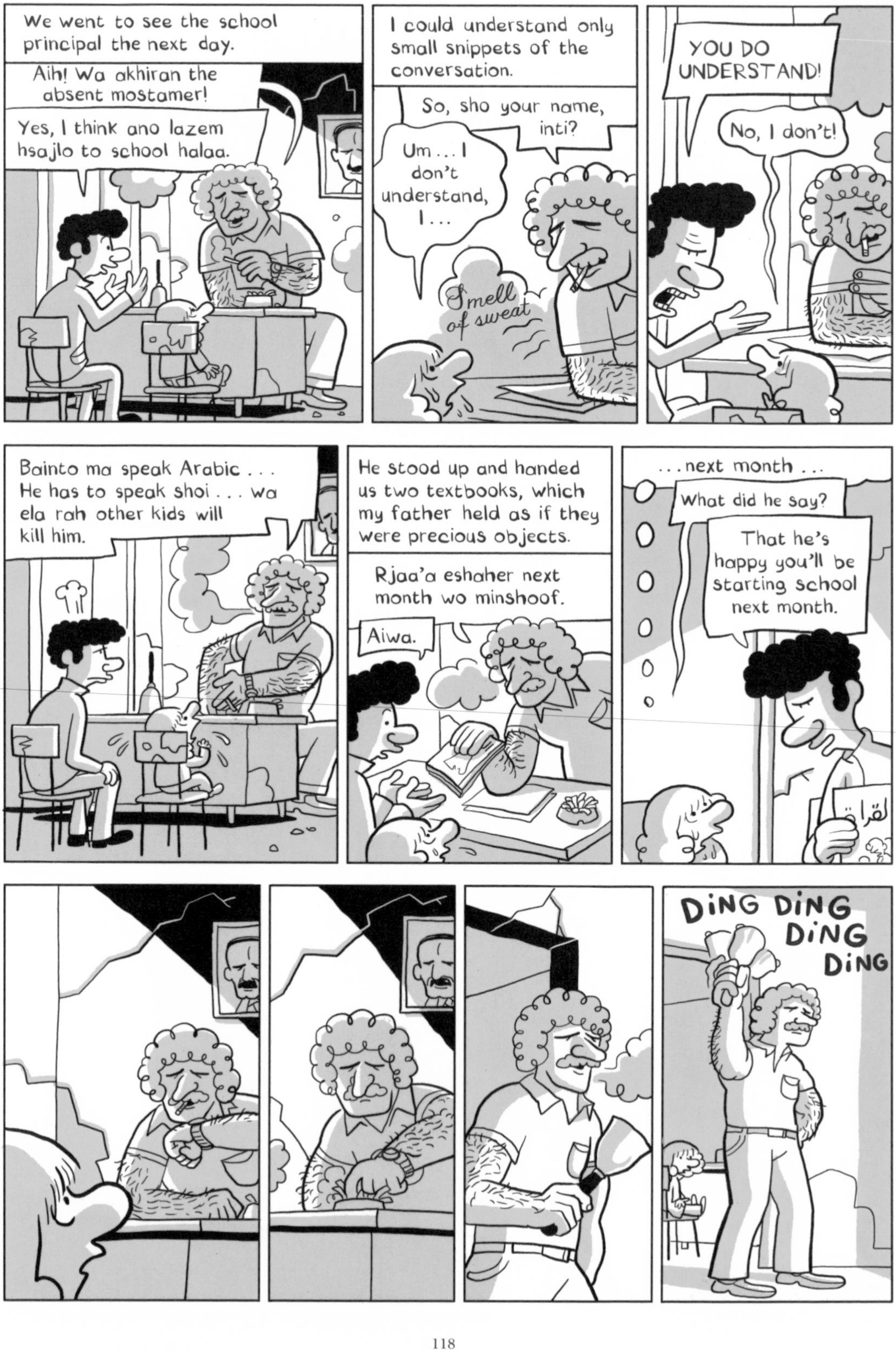
We went to see the school principal the next day.
Aih! Wa akhiran the absent mostamer!
Yes, I think ano lazem hsajlo to school halaa.
I could understand only small snippets of the conversation.
So, sho your name, inti?
Um . . . I don't understand, I . . .
Smell of sweat
YOU DO UNDERSTAND!
No, I don't!
Bainto ma speak Arabic . . . He has to speak shoi . . . wa ela rah other kids will kill him.
He stood up and handed us two textbooks, which my father held as if they were precious objects.
Rjaa'a eshaher next month wo minshoof.
Aiwa.
. . . next month . . .
What did he say?
That he's happy you'll be starting school next month.
DING DING DING DING

Following the sound of the bell, a huge deafening noise shook the building.
Ma'ha elsalameh, Doctor.
You see? He's a nice guy! But he was in the army before this, I think.
RRAAAARRRGGGHHH!
RRAARRGGHH!
Ahhh, school! How I used to love it!
We spotted Anas in the crowd.
Anas!
Give your father my best!
Anas is your age and he goes to school! You'll be in the same class.

Little by little, my Arabic improved, as I spent the afternoons with Wael and Mohamed whenever they didn't have classes.
Their apartment was exactly the same as ours
They didn't have the same toys as me, though.
Let's play war!
YEAH!
All their toys were kept in a little plastic bag.
Who wants the Syrian soldiers?
Me! Me!
Me, too.
The Syrian soldiers were made of molded green plastic, the same material as my cousins' shoes. They were all frozen in brave, heroic postures.
Crudely made
Kalashnikov
Communications officer
Sniper in hiding
All right, so you get the Jews.
Okay.
Pffft.
The Israeli soldiers were made of blue plastic. They were shaped in deceitful, treacherous poses.
Surrendering soldier
Made in China written underneath
Smooth reptilian face
Dagger
front view
back view
Dead soldier impaled by flag

It was hard to play with the soldiers. We couldn't bend them or change their positions, so there wasn't much to do with them.
?!?
Hey, let's set an ambush!
Yeah!
I've spotted a Jew right ahead of us, sir.
I see him, too ...
HANDS UP, JEW!
He's waving the white flag. He's surrendering, ha ha!
?
Watch out! He's holding a dagger behind his back!
We should execute him.
Yep.
Let's cut off his head.
Good idea.
My cousin sawed at the toy's neck until its head came off.
Victory is ours! God is great!
Ha ha!
WHAT ARE YOU DOING WITH THAT KNIFE?

I was cutting off the Jew's head! I'm allowed to do that!
WHAT?
YOU HEARD ME!
I'LL TEACH YOU TO BREAK YOUR TOYS! THEY COST GOOD MONEY!
I'LL TELL YOUR FATHER ABOUT THIS!
DON'T CARE!
He'll get torn apart for this . . .
HUFF! HUFF! He's going HUFF! to kill HUFF! me HUFF!
YAH!
TING
WAAH!
When evening came, all was calm.
The children sat against the wall and waited for the father to return.
Wael and Mohamed's father was one of Haj Mohamed's sons. He was a math teacher at the high school in the next village.
So... your grades?
10/10
Good.
10/10
Good.
I didn't get one.
Good.
10/10
Hmm.
He and my father (who was his uncle) got on very well: they were the only ones in the family to have gone to university.
Ah, thank you!

So, have you been good today?
Yes, Papa!
Yes, Papa!
Yes, Papa!
Yes, Papa!
WHACK
WHACK!
WHACK
WHACK
I HATE HAVING TO DO THAT!
WAAAAAAH!
One, never lie to your father! Two, always obey your mother! Three, don't decapitate your toys!
WAAAAAH!
SORRY PAPA!
WAA-AAAH!
And then, a few minutes later . . .
Here, eat this.
Come, it's over.
sniff
sniff

We were allowed to go outside but only up to the roof or just outside the porch.
You make two upside-down triangles.
The first one . . .
?
. . . and the second.
It's the Jewish star! URGH!
If you see a plane with this symbol, fire at it!
Our star is like this, and there are two of them.
Wait, rub out the Jews' star before you draw ours.
Huh! That's pretty good!
Secretly thrilled by the concept of triangles
Horrible! PTOO!
We had to observe certain superstitions.
Always look at the ground, in case you see a bit of bread.
?
Stale piece of bread
If you find one, you should pick it up and do this.
Mwaah
Then you put the bread on a wall or a rock, so it's not touching the ground.
The bread mustn't touch Satan.

If you see a shoe lying upside down ... you do this.

The soles of shoes have been touching the filthy earth.

You mustn't let them face God! You have to turn them to the earth, toward Satan.

The same goes for your own shoes!

Got it!

Watch out!

Actually, you're a star in my class!

Oh really?

Yeah, when the teacher does roll call, he says your name but you're never there!

The other kids think you always manage to play hooky!

You're their idol!

So the teacher says, "When that Sattouf comes back, I'm going to hit him so hard, it'll break my cane!"

WHAT??

HA HA HA HA!

HA HA HA HA!

Mohamed and Wael taught me every one of the basic Syrian insults.
"SON OF A DOG!" That's a good one, son of a dog.
SON OF A DOG!
You can use it at any time.
There's also "KISS MY ASS."
KISS MY ASS!
It means "NO." If a son of a dog asks you for something, say that.
Another one you can use all the time to insult anyone is "FUCK YOUR MOTHER!"
FUCK YOUR MOTHER!
But insults about fathers were always much more serious.
"A CURSE ON YOUR FATHER." You have to be careful with that one.
It's dangerous.
If you want to say it, you need to be sure you can beat up the guy you say it to. Because he'll definitely want to fight if you say "A CURSE ON YOUR FATHER."
A CURSE ON YOUR FATHER!
But you . . . you really need to be careful.
Ahem.
You could make an insult stronger by going back through the generations.
"A curse on your father's mother's father."
Whoah! That's a really nasty one!
Fuck your father's mother's mother's father.
Whoaah! Slow down!
Okay, now I'm going to tell you the worst one of all.
But you can never say it.
I shouldn't even tell you because it's so bad to say.
I'll whisper it in your ear.
"A curse . . . on . . . your . . . God . . ."
?

Of course, you can never say that to a Muslim.
You can only say it to a Christian or a Jew you're planning to kill.
Look, it's Anas and Moktar.
What are you doing here, you filthy Jew? I fuck your mother's mother's father!
Fuck your God, you filthy Jewish dog!
Don't you dare talk to Muslims, you filthy Jew!
Go screw your mother!
Anas and Moktar were younger than Mohamed and Wael, but Mohamed and Wael couldn't defend me because Anas and Moktar were their uncles.
And you! What the hell are you doing, hanging around with a Jew?
GRRR!
AAAAHHH!
!
RiAD!

YOU MUSTN'T FIGHT WITH YOUR FAMILY!
!!!
I explained to him that Anas had cursed my mother's father's God.
Maybe he did, but you must not retaliate! Never!
You must LOVE your family, love them more than yourself.
If I ever see you attacking them again, you'll be in big trouble!
What if they attack me?
Then you should run away! Don't get involved!
You're family!
A few days later . . .
WHAT ARE YOU DOING ON OUR ROOF, YOU FILTHY JEW?

Hello Uncles!
With your ugly yellow Jewish hair!
You've stolen our building! I fuck your whore mother's father's father!
Piss off! Go back to Israel!
Stop! We ... we're the same family. My father says we mustn't fight!
Something strange happened then. I wanted to retaliate, but instead I began to shake and laugh.
HA HA HA!
I wanted to disobey my father and beat them up, but I felt paralyzed.
HA HA HA HA HA!
When you come to school, we're going to kill you!
Waaaaah!
I fuck your mother's father's sister!

On Friday evenings, the TV news showed highlights of the president's prayers, which always took place in the morning.
Hafez al-Assad arrived in socks, followed by a mob of other shoeless men.
He glanced around suspiciously. There was no sound with the images other than the chanting of a sura from the Quran.
The president began the prayers. When he joined his hands together, the crowd behind him did the same.
He was the first to kneel . . .
. . . and nobody got up before he did.

You know who that is? It's President Assad.
Is he strong?
Very Strong!
He's a clever man!
Well, he's an Alawite, so he's not really a true Muslim, but still . . .
He came from a poor family . . . Back then, the Alawites lived in the mountains like wild animals.
Some of them were so poor they sold their children as slaves to the Sunnis.
And the Sunnis made them work like animals.
Can you just imagine? What if I sold you in exchange for a Mercedes, for example?
But Hafez al-Assad was able to go to school, and as he was excellent at math (not surprising, when you see the size of his head), he became a fighter pilot.
With hard work and determination, he was able to stage a coup and become president.
He seized his chance.
He gave all the important jobs to Alawites and now we are their slaves!

I didn't really grasp much of what he was saying, but I was fascinated by the way he was lying on the floor.
He held up his head with his arms.
I didn't understand how a person could stay in that position.
Heaviest head in the universe
And now for world news . . .
The defense minister of the Union of Soviet Socialist Republics affirmed his country's friendship and support for the Syrian Arab Republic . . .
. . . during a meeting with Hafez al-Assad, our eternal president. We will bring you those images now.
TV
Vivaldi's "Four Seasons" began playing.
There was no sound or commentary.
The Russian looked like a school child in class

My father muttered to himself while he watched.
What's a Jew, Papa?
What do you mean, what's a Jew?
The Jews are our enemies. They're occupying Palestine.
They're the worst race in the world. Well, them and the Americans, of course, who are their biggest pals . . .
Why are you telling him that? It's total crap . . .
A-ha! Look at your mother, she loves Jews! When I met her, she had all Enrico Macias's albums!
Don't deny it! You thought I looked like him!
Pffft.
HAHA
DIDN'T YOU?
Anas and Moktar say . . . they say that me and Mama are Jews.
You must have misunderstood. Not surprising, since you don't speak Arabic!

My father wanted to teach me to be more independent, so he sent me to take food to my grandmother.
I had to cross the street on my own . . .
VRRRROOOOM
. . . and avoid Anas and Moktar.
Beat it, you filthy Jew! You're not coming in here.
I've brought apples for Grandmother!
A curse on your father, you son of a bitch!
Get lost, Jew, or I'll beat the shit out of you!
I was often saved by one of their big brothers, who would usually sleep all day in a room near the entrance.
HEY! SHUT IT, WILL YOU? LET HIM PAST!
KNOCK KNOCK
Uhhh? Who is it? Oh, Riad! Come in, my sweet!
Come in and see your grandmother!

Big, slobbery kiss
Here, Grandma! We brought you some apples from Homs!
Oh, all these for me?
Grandma, why are you talking to that thief?
They stole our big house from us . . . He's a Jew, and so's his mother . . .
Ha ha.
Look! Riad brought you some fruit!
They deliberately bit into every single apple while staring at me . . .
CRUNCH
CRUNCH CRUNCH
. . . then threw them one by one on the carpet.
CRUNCH
My grandmother laughed and hugged them. I began to feel dizzy, so I left.
Hee hee!
CRUNCH CRUNCH

A few days later, I woke in the middle of the night, close to my mother.
She was watching my brother with a strange expression. There'd been another power outage.
I decided to call her.
RRRRRRRRRRRR
Startled from my nightmare, I saw a faceless figure moving in the darkness.
Open your mouth! Open your mouth!
?!!
You have to take your antibiotics.

I was very sick. I had a fever, and it wouldn't go away.
I tried six pharmacies. No luck. There are no more antibiotics to be had anywhere in Homs . . .
I even went to a store that takes dollars. But they were closed.
I'll try in Damascus tomorrow . . .
HNNN
COUGH! COUGH!
I . . . don't . . . want to go . . . to school . . . Anas is going to kill me . . .
Milking the situation
He's delirious from the fever
There are plenty of children in this village who get sick and don't have antibiotics!
AND THAT DOESN'T STOP THEM FROM GOING TO SCHOOL!

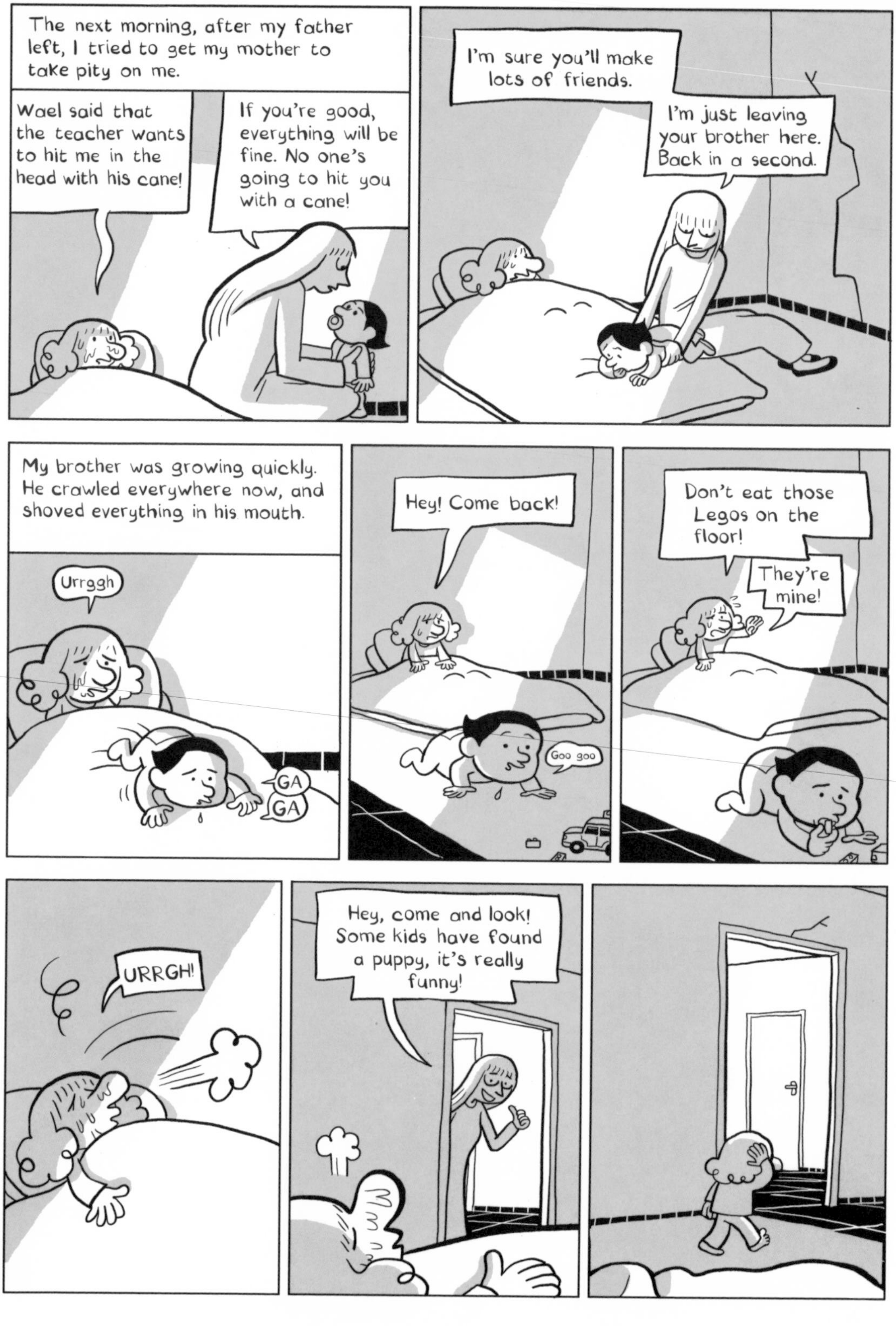
The next morning, after my father left, I tried to get my mother to take pity on me.
Wael said that the teacher wants to hit me in the head with his cane!
If you're good, everything will be fine. No one's going to hit you with a cane!
I'm sure you'll make lots of friends.
I'm just leaving your brother here. Back in a second.
My brother was growing quickly. He crawled everywhere now, and shoved everything in his mouth.
Urrggh
GA
GA
Hey! Come back!
Goo goo
Don't eat those Legos on the floor!
They're mine!
URRGH!
Hey, come and look! Some kids have found a puppy, it's really funny!

No one in the village kept a dog as a pet.
In Islamic tradition, dogs are considered unclean.
WOOF!
The dogs we heard at night were all strays, and they never went near people.
Li li li li!
The puppy must have been abandoned by its pack.
Aaahh!
HA HA
YAP!
What the hell are they doing?

They started playing soccer with it.
HAHA
They weren't kicking very hard.
Anas and Moktar were there. They were enjoying the show, but they kept their distance.
A few boys seemed to start yelling at something we couldn't see. They made themselves look fierce.
Grrrrr!
A curse on your father!
Was somebody there?
Moktar threw a rock at the puppy . . .
Yelp!
Ungh
Very good aim
. . . then an older boy appeared with a pitchfork and stabbed the dog with it.
CRUNCH
Look at my flag! HA HA HA!
HA HA
YELP
THEY'RE KILLING IT! WE HAVE TO DO SOMETHING!

My mother ran down to the street and I saw her trying to grab the pitchfork.
Then an old guy arrived and chopped off the puppy's head with a shovel.
THWACK
Ungh!
Two women gently approached my mother, who was going crazy.
Ha ha
Trying to calm her
Everyone was laughing. I wanted to go down to do something, but my fever had left me feeling too weak.
My brother was crawling across the floor of the hallway.
Hey! What are you doing?
He had found a roach's nest and was swallowing the eggs!
Goo goo?
More eggs near the wall
SLURP!
Yes! That's good! Eat all the roach eggs! Eat!
Mmgoo goo

After the incident with the dog, I wasn't allowed to leave the house.
Complete happiness
So the puppy did not die in vain.
Those kids heartlessly killed a dog, AND THEY THOUGHT IT WAS FUNNY!
He is not going to school with them. He's too young. Period. End of discussion!
So what? They're kids! Kids are like that! Pfft, all this fuss for a dog!
SLURP
You might have convinced your mother, but don't forget, you're not French, you're Syrian! And in Syria, boys take their father's side! Period.
Maybe you could teach me to read and write?
No. Better go and draw or play with your naked plastic men.
One day, my mother woke me in the middle of the night.
Wake up! Today's the day! We're finally going back to France!
Huh?
You heard me! Come on, grab your toys and pack your bag.
So, Anas and Moktar weren't going to kill me! I was saved!

CHAPTER 4

We flew back to France on Syrian Airlines.

Hello! Welcome aboard!

The captain was greeting people →

Hello, gorgeous!

Nice guy, but no teeth →

The flight attendants were unpleasant and never smiled.

Sweat

The plane was a Boeing 747 and had two levels. Upstairs, in first class, all the passengers were rich Syrians.

I'd never seen anything like them →

They all wanted to get there first.

True →

I'M VERY RICH, MOVE!

Go ahead darling, push in front!

Fuck your mother!

You son of a dog, do you know who I am?

Kiss my ass

In second class, where we were, smoking was allowed.

I had to sit separately from my parents, a few rows ahead.

I was sitting next to a German man.

The pilots on Syrian Airlines were ex-fighter pilots.
RRRRRRRR
They took off vertically . . .
AAAHHHH
. . . and straightened up within two seconds.
RRR
SCHEISSE
The German guy kept looking at me strangely and smiling.
He smoked his cigarette . . .
. . . and let loose some really vile farts.
PPRTTFFFFF
AAH
PRTTT
Are you German?
Perfect Arabic
Huh?
No, Syrian.
Hmm, you're a cute one, though, with your blond hair . . .
Are you traveling alone?
PFRRRT
NO.
He thought I was too young to realize he was the one making those evil farts.
PFFFFFFFF
AAAHH

A few hours later, the plane touched down (not quite on the runway) in Paris . . .
SYRIANAIR
ROAR!
. . . bounced up in the air . . .
SYRIANAIR
and then landed for good.
AAHHHHH!
BANG BANG BANG
AY AY AY AY AY!
GOD IS GREAT!
GOD IS GREEEAAAT!
BRAVO, PILOT!
GOD IS GREAT!
AY AY AY AY AY!
GOD IS GREAT!
CLAP CLAP CLAP CLAP CLAP
The German's ears were causing him terrible pain, because the airplane had descended so quickly.
Accchhhhh . . . !
AAH
Come, let's go!
ACH!
CRUNCH!
I stepped right on his balls. He probably thought that I didn't mean to do it.
Ha ha, son of a dog!

This time, my grandmother came to meet us at the airport.
The French air was spicy
She had remarried. Her new husband looked like an American actor.
Pleased to meet you, young man. I'm Charles, like the prince.
The first handshake of my life
But I'd like you to call me "Pappy."
Labass? Kif saha?
I speak a little Arabic. I lived in Morocco, do you know Morocco? I heard you speak Arabic . . .
Maybe it's not the same Arabic as in Morocco, huh?
How do you say "How are you?"
Hmm?
So, answer him! Say something! Speak Arabic!
It's okay, don't . . .
He is so STUPID!
Noo . . .
In Arabic, there are lots of sounds that don't exist in French. To me, it sounded like a person throwing up . . . So I was embarrassed to speak Arabic in front of strangers.
He's just shy . . .

We went to live in my grandmother's house.
We all slept in the same room.
Whoo
Whoo
It was summer and we went to the beach. My father kept bumping into people he knew.
Hey Abdel, how's it going? Been a long time. Where were you, in jail?
Ha ha
ha ha!
Large, muscular Breton
He would invite himself to play volleyball . . .
Hey! It's coming over!
Ha ha, careful, take cover!
He thought he was a great player.
Let me try again. I know I'll win this time!
Leave it to me, we're not messing around here !
WHAM!
After a while, no one would play with him. So he left the court in silence, pretending that nothing had happened.
Sniff

Bébette, the old woman who lived in the Middle Ages, had died. Her house was empty.
Come, let's go see the witch's house!
She was nice. She gave me cookies!
WHAT? PLEASE TELL ME YOU DIDN'T EAT THEM!
TELL ME THE TRUTH!
Um . . .
Um, no, I didn't eat any . . .
Phew! Because witches always give kids things to eat to cast a spell on them . . .
And then you're cursed with bad luck. Bad things happen . . .
You must always refuse food from strangers, especially women.
You know why? Because Satan likes to hide inside women.
It makes it easier for him to trick men.
Charles was interested in politics.
So, Abdel, what do you think of Gaddafi and Assad? Would you say that they're dictators?
Of course they're dictators! I'm not a moron! But it's different with Arabs . . .
You have to be tough with them. You have to force them to get an education, make them go to school . . . If they decide for themselves, they do nothing. They're lazy-ass bigots, even though they have the same potential as everyone else . . .

I'm the only one in my family who can read and write. School wasn't compulsory when I was young . . .
Gaddafi's not stupid. He's forcing the Arabs to change.
When the Arabs are educated, they'll free themselves from the old dictators . . .
And what will they get instead? Young dictators?
When I first met you, all you wanted to do was stage a coup!
HA HA! When I was young, there were coups every week! It's no surprise that I thought of doing one myself!
Seizing the opportunity, taking the decision that changes your life and that of everyone around you . . . Being the one who leads the coup . . .
I believe in freedom, but . . . the people have to choose . . . Westerners think the whole world should be exactly like them . . . Just because they're the most powerful . . .
But that's only temporary.
One day, I'll stage a coup d'état . . . and I'll have everyone killed.
Hee hee.

A few weeks later, we took the boat in Saint-Malo.
There was a huge storm during the crossing. All the passengers were sick except my father.
I've never been seasick . . .
Blurgh!
. . . because I was born to cross the ocean!
In return for the two years my father had worked in Libya, he had been paid $80,000 into an account based on the island of Jersey.
We ate three very disgusting hot dogs . . .
TOBACCONIST
CLEVER
SALE
. . . then he told us to wait for an hour.
EY
BANK
So we walked around Saint-Hélier. People's bodies here were very strange.
Women's breasts were lower than normal

After an hour, my father joined us at the port.
Guess what? Now I'm a rich man! I have $30,000 in my pocket!
The cleanest ground in the world
Hee hee! Have you ever seen dollars? The best currency in the world, look!
Beautiful dollars!
I'll hide them under my belt. That way, French customs won't find them!
Nor Syrian customs, for that matter!
Hee hee
I know the last year in Syria was hard, but everything will be better now . . .
?
Next week, with this money, I can start construction on my luxury villa, on my land . . .
!?!?!
We . . . we're going back to Syria?
Of course! The summer's nearly over . . . You can't spend your whole life on vacation!
The Arab of the future goes to school!
7

Riad Sattouf 2014

ABOUT THE AUTHOR

RIAD SATTOUF is a bestselling cartoonist and filmmaker who grew up in Syria and Libya and now lives in Paris. The author of four comics series in France and a former contributor to the satirical publication *Charlie Hebdo*, Sattouf is now a weekly columnist for *l'Obs*. He also directed the films *The French Kissers* and *Jacky in the Women's Kingdom*. *The Arab of the Future*, which has been translated into sixteen languages, is his first work to appear in English.